POTLUCK!

HOME COOKING FROM WISCONSIN'S COMMUNITY COOKBOOKS

TONI BRANDEIS STRECKERT

TRAILS BOOKS
Madison, Wisconsin

Library of Congress Control Number: 2007936918
ISBN: 978-1-931599-88-7

Portions of this book originally appeared in the *Wisconsin State Journal* and are reprinted with permission.

Editor: Mark Knickelbine
Designer: Colin Harrington

Printed in the United States of America by Sheridan Books.

12 11 10 09 08 07   6 5 4 3 2 1

Trails Books, a division of Big Earth Publishing
923 Williamson Street • Madison, WI 53703
(800) 258-5830 • www.trailsbooks.com

DEDICATION

To my father who taught me the value of the past;
to my mother who taught me the value of change; and to my husband,
for his usual good cheer and support through all my
often terrifying culinary experiments over the years.

TABLE OF
CONTENTS

ACKNOWLEDGMENTS

Recipes, by their nature, link you to a community of cooks and customs; and when you're working with thousands of family recipes, your community quickly becomes quite large. To fully credit all those who helped bring this project to fruition would be to require the reader to traverse many pages, a prospect that brings to mind a quote from the famous British barrister and judge, Lord Birkett, who stated: "I do not object to people looking at their watches when I am speaking. But I strongly object when they start shaking them to make certain they are still going."

Nevertheless, this cookbook could not have been realized without many hands stirring the pot, and an abundance of cooks, past and present, in the kitchen. I would like to hoist a 21-spatula salute to the wonderful test cooks, who painstakingly reviewed and tried out recipes, made notes, and demonstrated the perfect balance of level headedness, levity, and leavening to see this project through. They were often give a time frame to prepare entrees that was tighter than a new pair of pointy-heeled shoes. Among them are Mary Ales, Beth Billingham, Becky Buchmann, Syndi Dobson, Merija Eisen, Marybeth Friske, Laura Holt, Melissa Huggins, Susan Kau, Sue Knapp, Heidi Ness, Belinda Payne, Kim Pedracine, Robin Pettersen, Jill Reschke, Gino Segre, Pat Schumacher, Denise Thornton, Helen Valenta, Teri Woods, and Randy Zirk. A special thanks is also due Peggy Hager, who cooked up a storm and was an invaluable help in screening heritage and ethnic recipes. Gratitude is also due to my daughter, Emma Streckert, for preparing many, many dishes; her emerging baking abilities were honed during this project, and her advanced dishwashing skills were sorely tested during the research stage of this book. Her friends—Libby Ales, Sally Cole, Mira Hager, Melanie Reschke, Lauren Pedracine, and Jennifer Zirk—also test-baked recipes and provided valuable recipe feedback and input, particularly for the dessert section.

Deborah Thorp, Rich Lampert, Tom Andersen, and Harry Streckert (yes, I pressed all family members into service) aided immeasurably with consultation and technical support.

Beth Weber and Jeff Horney were always available for help in culling and interpreting recipes, and Sara Plath generously assisted with her piece on the role of community cookbooks in our culture. Leanne Lobravico, Kate Gallagher, Bob and Nancy Hilf, Jamie Klubertanz, Ye-Yeng Wang, Dave Streckert, and the extended Streckert family provided ongoing support and encouragement. Carole and Dan Doeppers were cheerfully available 24/7 for taste testing and recipe evaluation. And finally, a very special thank you to SSK, a special friend of Josephine Adamowski's, for her labor-intensive and overwhelming aid in all aspects of this book.

Since this book was written, I regret to note the untimely death of one of the recipe testers, Becky Buchmann, a woman who was as warm and generous with her friendship and cooking as she was toward the many young people (and others) she worked with and encouraged at Madison's Cherokee Middle School library. There is a saying attributed to Buddha that could well be applied to Becky: *Fashion your life as a garland of beautiful deeds.*

INTRODUCTION

Our experience of food is rich with memory and emotional bonds. A favorite recipe or dish can trigger a world of reminiscence and ancestral history. Some recipes function as part of a rich oral tradition, and are a link to previous generations; this is particularly true in Wisconsin, which has such strong and vital historic connections. We have, right in our midst, vintage treasures that are accessible to all and yet are too often overlooked in our quest to find pieces of the past. These bits of living, still-unfolding history can be discovered in the recipes found between the pages of community cookbooks.

The recipes are also a part of our history that for the most part have been handed down by women, by mothers and aunts and grandmothers, dear neighbors and old friends, and friends of friends. They are time capsules of how we lived and ate through the decades—from the butter cookies, mincemeat pies, and *lefse* that date to the turn of the twentieth century—to our present day culinary interest in pesto, curry, feta cheese, and exotic mushrooms.

The potluck recipes in this book that come from church and community cookbooks span both worlds. Many feature new combinations of fresh Wisconsin produce with natural ingredients, reflecting today's cooking trends while at the same time honoring the past. A fortunate trend in these small, locally produced cookbooks is the appearance of sections devoted to ethnic, traditional, or "heritage" cooking, accompanied often with old photographs and a line or two of reminisce. It is quite easy to get entirely absorbed in these cookbooks and try to read between the lines and tablespoons to glimpse the women who transmitted their own poetry over the years through cookie doughs, breads, casseroles, and pie crusts.

Except for some of the recipes in the Heritage and Ethnic Specialties and Extra Helpings chapters, the overwhelming majority of the recipes in this book were test baked and tried. This involved a community experience in its own right; more than 20 cooks helped out in preparing dishes. I solicited multiple opinions for each recipe to account for the vagaries of individual palates. I sought suggestions for variations as well, which are included at the end of the recipes; and if the author of the original recipe included a note, I distinguished those notes from the rest.

For many of the test cooks, myself included, the most difficult part of this enterprise was to punctiliously follow the recipes, particularly the struggle to avoid adding or reducing certain ingredients. For some of us, this was an almost painful experience at times; I had never realized how much of the essence of one's personality and strongly held, though often unvoiced, nutritional and culinary belief system comes out in the manner in which we prepare a recipe. And just as families and friends want the best outcomes for their children and those of others, the testers approached their recipes with the same open-hearted and open-handed attitude, though on occasion even with the most thoughtful preparation and solicitous suggestions for improvement, the entree could not be saved. As in the case of many of the kitchen's intermittent disappointments, the best remedy was usually to move on to the next dish.

As this small army of cooks reviewed hundreds of recipes, the ground rule for inclusion in this book was that the recipe had to have *at least one* of the following characteristics:

- ▶ It was handed down through families or friends;
- ▶ It uses fresh or natural ingredients;
- ▶ It reflects either our immigrant or Wisconsin regional backgrounds;
- ▶ It is either unique, or a great version of a traditional recipe—such as a lemon pie;
- ▶ One would proudly bring the dish to a potluck.

In the 14 cookbooks that these recipes are drawn from, there were countless variations on certain worthy recipes, such as molasses cookies, chili, lemon and apple pies, rhubarb desserts, and beef stews. We typically tried many versions of these recipes, and it often was a balancing act to choose from among several equally delicious renditions of them. The final decision to include a recipe was based on ease of preparation, quality of ingredients, the authenticity and uniqueness of the recipe, the "age" of the recipe to insure a mix of both heritage and contemporary dishes, and finally, that certain highly gratifying and often difficult to define joining of flavors that heralds the arrival of a serious potluck player. We wanted to fairly represent all the chosen cookbooks, and had space considerations to keep in mind as well.

One of the most fun and rewarding parts of assembling this book was holding potlucks to evaluate the recipes. I would suggest a "recipe potluck" with friends to anyone who needs to refresh their spirit and outlook. At times I felt like the female equivalent of George Bailey in the last act of *It's a Wonderful Life*, surrounded by a community of friends, neighbors, and acquaintances, most generously dispensing their time, cooking talents, advice, and critiques (and usually some very yummy food). In preparation for this book, we held recipe potluck tastings and evaluations for vegetarians, potlucks for book-club members (we each tried out one of the possible recipes for the cookbook and then rated them), and many Friday night and "work-in-progress" potluck dinners with friends and extended family. Because the stipulation was to fastidiously follow the recipe, everyone was free to openly express their opinion without stepping on the ego of the chef; some lively exchanges were held on the merits of shortening vs. butter in certain types of cooking, the all-critical mayo ratio in some appetizers, and the often fine line between having a perfect melding of flavors and being too bland. It made for quite engaging mealtime conversation and camaraderie, and we all got to feel like the judges on an entertainment show (though less pointlessly nasty, I hope), bent on grooming the next great talent.

I would like to extend a special thank you to all of the community cookbook and potluck coordinators and committee members who very generously shared some of their life stories and well-honed cooking tips with me. I'm especially grateful to Mary Christenson, who helped me understand the connection between traditional, small community cooking and some of the newer potluck influences of organic family farms and sustainable local agriculture. In one of our conversations, Mary told me, "Potlucks are a great way to build a community and get to know people. You get in the kitchen and get going. You feel that comfort level. It's something that everyone needs." That became one of two observations that greatly aided me in developing this book. The other was from my friend, Sara Plath, a writer and technology consultant whose work necessitates frequent travel throughout the country, and who first made me aware of the mother lode of experience found in church and community cookbooks. "You can trace the history of a community and the immigrant experience of the previous century in these recipes, and in the titles and anecdotes that go with them," she said

One caveat. I have had nightmare visions of a phalanx of disgruntled midwestern cookbook committee representatives, each angrily brandishing their own recipe book and demanding to know why their efforts were not represented in this collection. So to address these real or imagined concerns, I must clarify that for manageability I had to limit myself to 14 cookbooks—which together literally contained thousands of recipes. The books had to have been published within the last few years, and they were culled from books that had been submitted to the *Wisconsin State Journal* for its annual year-end round up of Wisconsin community cookbooks. This book is not intended to be a "best of" listing—or a cookbook popularity contest. The idea is to celebrate all of these great little recipe books and experience the ways our community and our history are expressed and strengthened through the dishes we bring to gatherings. While I wasn't able to include each of the hundreds of community cookbooks published throughout

Wisconsin, I hope this book will encourage you to support them and discover some of the wonderful old and new traditions between their covers. Seek out these spiral-bound treasures where you live and travel, then purchase one or two of them and pass them on as gifts to yourself and others. For a reasonable price, you can have your own bit of history to hand down, and also give to a good cause in the process.

Ordering information for the cookbooks featured in this book can be found in the Contributing Cookbooks section; the recipes featured herein represent a very small portion of their gems.

—Toni Brandeis Streckert

APPETIZERS

ON THE VALUE OF COMMUNITY COOKBOOKS

Sara Plath, New York writer and (enthusiastic) amateur cook

I grew up in Iowa with the kind of cookbooks represented in *PotLuck!* My aunts would get them from churches. I've bought community cookbooks wherever I've found them in my travels around the United States. I've always been fascinated by what these books say about this country, and these recipes speak to me of immigrants, of tastes and cultures brought along with the sack or suitcase, the mingling and transformation on American soil. In almost all of these cookbooks you can find recipes that reflect what's left of true regional and ethnic American immigrant cooking.

Cookbooks from the West and Southwest show the old layer of Spanish and Mexican influence. Enslaved Africans brought seeds for pigeon peas, black-eyed peas and okra, and founded one American way of cooking. The Italians and the Portuguese brought their seafood stews to the towns of the Northeast along with their fishing skills. In cookbooks from Wyoming, you'll find the Basque heritage intact in lamb roasts and breads. The oldest layer is what was already here—the plants, vegetables, and ways of cultivating that early immigrants learned from the Native Americans. In the Pacific Northwest, for instance, immigrants learned from the locals how to cook salmon on a cedar plank.

Community cookbooks are a treasury of good, practical cooking that grew up with the ingredients of a particular place and time: the gumbos of the South, the green-chili stews of New Mexico, the Brunswick stews of North Carolina, the Scandinavian pastries in cookbooks from Minnesota. This is who we are, how we got here, what we found, what we made of it. These aren't the cookbooks of three-hour reductions and fancy garnishes and ingredients from another continent; at their best, they are about good cooking using local knowledge and local ingredients.

If I'm inclined to make a cabernet reduction (and I have the three hours), I have excellent professional cookbooks to go to. If I'm contemplating the perfect fried chicken, I go to my community cookbooks; I can find a dozen renditions, each of them perfect in their own way.

GREAT GARLIC CHEESE BREAD

1 large loaf French or sourdough bread
2 to 3 cloves garlic, crushed
$1/2$ pound rope or shredded provolone cheese
$1/4$ cup half & half
1 to 2 tablespoons minced parsley

Slice bread into 1 to 1 1/2-inch slices, cutting all the way through. Combine the remaining ingredients. Mix well. Spread between slices. Wrap loaf lightly in foil and leave venting at top of foil. Bake in preheated 400-degree oven for 20 to 25 minutes. Serve warm.

Barb Van Der Hulst, Evelyn Beyer
Cooksville Lutheran Church Cookbook

Kids love this, though adults might want to substitute their favorite sharp cheese for the provolone or use half sharp cheese and half provolone.

LEMON PARMESAN ARTICHOKE BOTTOMS

$1/2$ cup Parmesan cheese, grated
$1/2$ cup regular or reduced-fat mayonnaise
3 large garlic cloves, minced
2 teaspoons fresh lemon juice
1 teaspoon lemon peel, grated
Salt and pepper, to taste
2 cans (14 ounces each) of artichoke crowns or bottoms, rinsed,
    drained, and patted dry
$1/4$ cup pine nuts

Combine all ingredients except the artichoke bottoms and pine nuts. Mound onto artichoke bottoms. Sprinkle with pine nuts. Bake at 375 degrees in a lightly greased baking dish for 20 minutes or until heated through. Makes 14-16 servings.

Debbie Sherraden
Sharing Our Recipes: A Collection by the Park Elementary School PTA, Cross Plains

CRANBERRY DIP (HOT AND SPICY)

1 can (16 ounces) jellied cranberry sauce
3 tablespoons prepared horseradish
2 tablespoons honey
1 tablespoon Worcestershire sauce
1 tablespoon lemon juice
1 clove garlic, minced
$1/_2$ teaspoon cayenne pepper

Combine the cranberry sauce, horseradish, honey, Worcestershire sauce, lemon juice, garlic, and cayenne pepper in a medium saucepan and mix well. Bring to a boil; reduce the heat. Simmer, covered, for 5 minutes. Serve warm with orange sections, pineapple cubes, or sausages. Makes 1 1/2 cups.

From Our House to Your House: Recipes from the Madison Curling Club

---

LEMON GARLIC SHRIMP

2 $^1/_2$ pounds large cooked shrimp, peeled and deveined
2 small red onions, thinly sliced
4 large lemons, thinly sliced, seeds removed
2 teaspoons crushed fresh rosemary
4 garlic cloves, minced
1 bottle (32 ounces) olive oil
Juice of 2 lemons
Lettuce for lining serving bowl

Layer the shrimp, onion, and lemon slices in a large nonmetallic bowl. Sprinkle each layer with rosemary and garlic. Pour olive oil over layers until the top layer is covered. Drizzle with a little lemon juice. Cover and let marinate in refrigerator for 2 days, stirring occasionally. To serve, discard lemon slices and onions. Scoop out into a lettuce-lined bowl and serve with picks.

The Collection II: Simple & Elegant Recipes
Attic Angel Association

This special occasion treat will wow everyone. Be sure to plan enough time in advance so it can fully marinate.

THOUGHTS ON COOKING

Dorothy Traisman, Cookbook Committee Co-Chair
The Collection II: Simple & Elegant Recipes, Attic Angel Association

COOKING TIPS

▶ Check your spices' shelf life and replace them every 3 to 6 months. Chili powder especially will get darker and lose flavor, as it gets older.

▶ Try to avoid cooking that requires a lot of sugar on damp days. The sugar will absorb any additional moisture and get too grainy.

▶ Always read through the recipe completely before you start to avoid surprises.

My mother made super caramel bars and butterscotch brownies even though she didn't really like to cook. I think because of this, I started cooking myself at a fairly young age. Instead of just making peanut-butter sandwiches, I wanted to make tuna salad ones, cut into fancy shapes. I did a lot of cooking at home and had my share of early cooking mistakes, such as measuring the salt over the soup pot and spilling it. I also learned how to salvage cooking problems, such as changing jams or jellies that wouldn't set right into sundae toppings, or turning failed cakes into puddings. As I grew up, I was very active in the 4H and Future Homemakers of America organizations, and eventually I became a dietician and taught others for many years. My interest in cooking is still strong, and I read cookbooks the same way other people read fiction.

Our Attic Angels cookbook comes from a big cross section of our members. We were looking for interesting and satisfying recipes and tested most of them two and three times. More than half of the dishes are family favorites that were handed down. Our cookbook also features ample selections of desserts and appetizers—what most people look for first in a cookbook. We wanted to give them this and raise money for a good cause at the same time.

APPLE, PECAN, AND BLUE CHEESE DIP

    1 package (8 ounces) softened cream cheese
    1/2 cup sour cream
    1 Rome Beauty apple, finely chopped
    1/4 cup blue cheese
    1/4 cup red onion, finely chopped
    1/4 cup pecans, finely chopped

Mix all ingredients together, cover, and refrigerate at least 2 hours. Serve with crackers. Makes 24 servings.

Helen Anderson
Recipes and Memories, Trinity Lutheran Church, Arkdale

TOMATO TART

    Piecrust, partially baked (5–7 minutes)
    1 1/2 cup mozzarella cheese
    4 Roma tomatoes cut in wedges, drained
    3/4 cup basil leaves, chopped
    4 garlic cloves, minced
    1/2 cup mayonnaise
    1/4 cup Parmesan cheese
    Salt and pepper

Put 1/2 cup of mozzarella on piecrust. Arrange tomatoes over cheese. Mix basil and garlic; then combine with rest of mozzarella, mayonnaise, and grated Parmesan. Spread this mixture over tomato wedges and season with salt and pepper. Bake at 375 degrees for 25 minutes.

Shirley Brandt
For Everything There is a Season, Vermont Lutheran Church, 150 Years of Faith, Fellowship and Food

This has a delicious and strong basil flavor; it's just as good with light, low-fat mayonnaise.

RICOTTA PUFFS

1 package (17.3 ounces) frozen puff pastry (2 sheets), thawed
$^1/_2$ cup ricotta cheese
$^1/_2$ cup chopped roasted red sweet pepper
3 tablespoons grated Romano cheese
1 tablespoon snipped fresh parsley
1 teaspoon dried oregano, crushed
$^1/_2$ teaspoon ground black pepper
Milk

Unfold puff pastry on a lightly floured surface. Cut each pastry sheet into nine 3-inch squares; set aside. To make filling, in a medium bowl, stir together ricotta cheese, roasted pepper, Romano cheese, parsley, oregano, and black pepper. Moisten the edges of each pastry square with milk. Spoon about 2 teaspoons filling onto one side of each pastry square. Fold the other side of the pastry over the filling. Seal with the tines of a fork. Cut slits in top of each pastry bundle. Brush with milk; sprinkle with additional Romano cheese. Arrange pastry bundles on a baking sheet. Bake at 400 degrees for about 20 minutes or until golden. Cool on wire rack for 5 minutes before serving. Makes 18 pastries.

From Our House to Your House: Recipes from the Madison Curling Club

These are easier to make than they appear and make a very impressive-looking appetizer.

FROM OUR HOUSE TO YOUR HOUSE: THE CURLING TRADITION OF POTLUCKS

Bonnie Kees, Madison Curling Club

from Our House

to Your House

Recipes from
The Madison Curling Club

"The grand old game" of curling is an enjoyable winter recreation played on ice and is often passed down through families. The Madison Curling Club was founded in 1921 by William G. "Bill" McKay; curling is now a world and Olympic sport. Some say the term "curling" refers to the twist of the stone's handle upon release that makes it curve, or curl, as it travels down the ice.

The cookbook title, *From Our House to Your House*, contains a pun: the scoring area, which consists of a bull's-eye series of circles, is called the "house." The

MCC is rich in celebrations and hosts many state and national play-down events. Typically, teams are led to the playing surface, called the icehouse, by bag pipers. The camaraderie that follows a game ends with a potluck dish and tales of the game—a big tradition in curling known as broomstacking. The term refers to the social get-together between opponents after each game. Originally, after completing a curling game on the pond, curlers would stack their brooms in front of the fire and enjoy food and beverages with the opponent. This tradition is still very much alive today; curlers are expected to partake in broomstacking after every game. The recipes in the MCC cookbook come from some of the wonderful potluck dishes members prepare and enjoy at curling clubs.

The traditions and memories of the MCC members are shared through cooking. The first of the Ten Commandments of a Curler keeps the tradition alive: "Thou shalt have no other game before me, for I am the roarin' game which was in the beginning (even in the stone age), is now and ever shall be."

PEPPERONI BISCOTTI

$1/3$ cup butter, softened

$1/4$ cup plus 2 tablespoons grated Parmesan cheese, divided

1 tablespoon sugar

4 cloves garlic, minced

1 teaspoon baking powder

1 teaspoon dried Italian seasoning, crushed

1 egg

1 tablespoon milk

1 $1/2$ cups all-purpose flour

$1/2$ cup chopped pepperoni

$1/4$ cup finely chopped red sweet pepper

2 tablespoons finely chopped onion

2 tablespoons snipped fresh parsley

Lightly grease a baking sheet; set aside. In a large bowl, beat butter with an electric mixer on medium to high speed for 30 seconds. Add the 1/4 cup Parmesan cheese, sugar, garlic, baking powder, and Italian seasoning. Beat until combined. Beat in egg and milk. Beat in as much flour as you can with the mixer. By hand, stir in the remaining flour, pepperoni, red pepper, onion, and parsley.

Knead dough gently until it clings together. Shape into two 9-by-1 $1/2$-inch rolls. Roll dough rolls in the 2 tablespoons Parmesan cheese to coat. Place rolls on the prepared baking sheet; flatten slightly. Bake in 350-degree oven for 20 to 25 minutes or until a wooden toothpick inserted near center comes out clean.

Cool on sheet for 1 hour. Cut each roll crosswise into $^3/_4$-inch slices. Place slices, cut-sides down, on an ungreased baking sheet. Bake in 325-degree oven for 20 to 22 minutes more or until dry and crisp, turning once. (Do not overbake.) Transfer to a wire rack; cool. Makes about 24 biscotti.

From Our House to Your House: Recipes from the Madison Curling Club

This is labor intensive but well worth it—both unique and tasty.

DOUBLE SESAME ZUCCHINI STICKS

2 tablespoons sesame seeds

1 tablespoon sesame oil

1 teaspoon lemon juice

$^1/_4$ teaspoon salt

2 cups zucchini cut in julienne sticks (about 1 $^1/_2$-inches long, $^1/_4$-inch thick)

In a small, non-stick sauté pan, brown sesame seeds in sesame oil. Add zucchini, sprinkled with lemon juice and salt. Stir-fry until zucchini is as tender or crisp as you like. Makes 4 servings.

Helen Bannan
The Wisconsin Gardener Cookbook 3

BASIL LEEK APPETIZER

1 package (10 ounces) refrigerated pizza dough

6 medium leeks, thinly sliced

3 cloves garlic, minced

2 tablespoons olive oil

1 teaspoon dried basil or 2 tablespoons fresh basil, chopped

2 tablespoons Dijon mustard

1 tablespoon water

1 cup shredded Swiss or Gruyère cheese

$^1/_4$ cup toasted almonds or pine nuts

Preheat oven to 425. Unroll pizza dough on a greased baking sheet to make a 9-by-12-inch rectangle. Bake 7 minutes. Cool slightly. Meanwhile cook leeks and garlic in olive oil for 5 minutes. Remove from heat and stir in basil. Stir mustard and water together. Spread mustard mixture over crust. Top with leek mixture, cheese, and nuts. Bake 8 minutes until cheese is bubbly. Let stand 5 minutes. Cut into squares.

Klover Schafer
For Everything There is a Season, Vermont Lutheran Church, 150 Years of Faith, Fellowship and Food

Try rolling the crust out as flat and thin as possible. In addition, use as much of the leek as possible to have enough for this recipe.

MARINATED ZUCCHINI AND MUSHROOMS

8 small whole fresh mushrooms
2 small zucchinis or yellow squash, sliced into half inch slices (2 cups)
1 small red pepper sliced into squares ($^1/_2$ cup)
1 clove fresh garlic, minced
$^1/_4$ cup lemon juice
2 tablespoons olive oil
1 teaspoon sugar
$^1/_4$ teaspoon salt
$^1/_4$ teaspoon dried tarragon or oregano, crushed
$^1/_4$ teaspoon pepper

Place mushrooms, zucchini, and red pepper in a plastic bag set in a large bowl. For marinade, in a small bowl, mix garlic, lemon juice, oil, sugar, salt, tarragon or oregano, and pepper. Pour marinade over vegetables in bag and seal. Marinate in the refrigerator for 8 hours or overnight, turning bag occasionally.

To serve, pour vegetables and marinade into serving dish; serve with toothpicks.

Carla Lynch
From Our House to Your House: Recipes from the Madison Curling Club

---

STUFFED MUSHROOMS

10 medium mushrooms, firm, closed caps
1 tablespoon butter
2 tablespoons minced onion or green onion
$^1/_4$ cup breadcrumbs
$^1/_4$ cup shredded sharp cheddar cheese
2 tablespoons water
Salt and pepper to taste

Preheat oven to 350 degrees. Wash mushrooms quickly under running water, drain on paper towels. Pull stems from mushrooms and chop finely. Melt butter in a skillet over medium-low heat. Add chopped mushroom stems and onion. Sauté until tender. Stir in breadcrumbs, cheese, salt and pepper. Sprinkle salt over mushroom caps and fill with sautéed mixture, mounding over the top. At this point you may cover and refrigerate these mushrooms for up to 24 hours. Before serving, put 2 tablespoons of water in a shallow dish and arrange stuffed mushrooms in dish. Bake for about 20 minutes. Serve hot.

Maureen Karlstad
Pleasant Fridge: Pleasant Ridge Waldorf School Community Cookbook

There are many stuffed mushroom recipes around, but this simple one is top notch!

IDA'S SWISS ZUCCHINI ROUNDS

$^1/_3$ cup biscuit baking mix (like Bisquick)
$^1/_2$ teaspoon salt
$^1/_8$ teaspoon pepper
$^1/_3$ cup grated Swiss cheese
2 eggs, beaten
2 cups zucchini, shredded
2 to 3 tablespoons butter

In a mixing bowl, combine biscuit mix, salt, pepper, and cheese. Stir in eggs until mixture is moistened. Fold in zucchini. In a 10-inch skillet, melt butter over medium heat. Drop 2 tablespoons of batter in pan for each round. Cook 2 to 3 minutes per side or until nicely browned. Keep warm while preparing remaining round. Yield: 12 rounds.

Recipe is easily doubled. Great warm or cold.

Jocelyn Kline
Old World Swiss Family Recipes, Monroe Swiss Singers

BLT BITES

16 to 20 cherry tomatoes (or more if using smaller tomatoes)
1 pound bacon, cooked and crumbled
$^1/_2$ cup mayonnaise or salad dressing
$^1/_3$ cup chopped green onions
3 tablespoons Parmesan cheese
2 tablespoons snipped fresh parsley

Cut a thin slice off of each tomato top. Scoop out and discard pulp. Invert the tomatoes on a paper towel to drain. In a small bowl, combine the remaining ingredients; mix well. Spoon into tomatoes. Refrigerate for several hours.

Debbie Wheeler
United Presbyterian Church 150th Anniversary Cookbook

SALMON LOAF

2 cans salmon (about 2 cups)
2 eggs
Liquid from salmon and milk to make 1 $\frac{1}{2}$ cups
3 cups coarse cracker crumbs
2 tablespoons lemon juice
2 teaspoons chopped onion
$\frac{1}{4}$ teaspoon salt
$\frac{1}{4}$ teaspoon pepper

Preheat oven to 350 degrees. Flake salmon (remove bones if desired—they are also good left in). Blend with the rest of the ingredients. Spoon lightly into a 9x5x3-inch loaf pan. Bake for 45 minutes. Yield: 8 servings.

Every time I make this recipe, I remember my friend, Henrietta Kile. When she made this recipe for garden club potlucks, there were never leftovers.

Clara Thompson
The Catholic Communities of St. Andrew, Verona, and St. William, Paoli, Cookbook

---

BRAUNSCHWEIGER SPREAD

8 ounces braunschweiger, at room temperature
8 ounces of cream cheese, at room temperature
2 green onions, chopped
2 boiled eggs, chopped
Dash of Worcestershire sauce
$\frac{1}{2}$ to $\frac{3}{4}$ teaspoon horseradish
$\frac{1}{2}$ cup salad dressing, e.g., Miracle Whip

Combine all ingredients and mix well with a mixer. Refrigerate. Serve with crackers, toast, or rye bread. This can also be formed into a ball.

Dawn Nelson
Family and Friends Cuisine, 2006. A Collection of Favorite Recipes from the Family and Friends of Willerup United Methodist Church

The horseradish and Worcestershire sauce can be increased (and salad dressing omitted) for a zestier flavor. Hot pepper sauce can also be added.

FRESH CORN SALSA

4 cups corn, or 6 good-sized ears of corn (4 cups kernels)
1 red bell pepper, roasted and chopped
1 large tomato, chopped
2 jalapeño peppers, seeded and minced
1 bunch green onions, diced, tops and bottoms discarded ($^1/_2$ cup)

Mix ingredients together in large nonmetallic container. Don't worry about the salsa being too hot; the corn absorbs both heat and spice.

Dressing:

2 teaspoons medium chili powder
$^1/_2$ teaspoon dried cilantro (or 1 to 2 teaspoons fresh, chopped cilantro)
$^1/_2$ teaspoon garlic granules (or 2 cloves fresh)
$^1/_4$ teaspoon black pepper
2 tablespoons water
$^1/_4$ cup fresh lime juice (2 small limes)
$^1/_3$ cup corn oil
2 teaspoons sugar
1 teaspoon salt, divided

To make the dressing: Mix the chili powder, cilantro, garlic, and black pepper with 2 tablespoons water in a small bowl. Let stand 5 minutes. Add lime juice, oil, sugar, and 1/2 teaspoon salt. Whisk together to combine, and pour over corn mixture. Refrigerate overnight. Just before serving, toss again. Taste and adjust seasoning to your liking (add 1/2 teaspoon salt if needed). Serve with corn chips.

Kristin Mitchell
The Catholic Communities of St. Andrew, Verona, and St. William, Paoli, Cookbook

If desired, substitute cilantro for dried coriander. To roast a pepper, place ripe pepper on burner over medium-high heat. The pepper will start to blacken after 1 $^1/_2$ minutes. Using tongs, turn pepper, giving each side time to blacken. Let set for 15 minutes. Remove skin (run under cold water), core, remove seeds, and chop.

RHUBARB JUICE

    5 cups fresh rhubarb, chopped
    1 1/2 cups sugar
    8 cups water
    Juice of 2 fresh lemons (or use bottled)

Boil rhubarb and water until rhubarb is tender. Strain through a colander. Add sugar and lemon to juice and heat to boiling. Cool and keep in refrigerator. It can be frozen as well.

Pam Kaehn
Recipes and Memories, Trinity Lutheran Church

A fantastic and unusual spring and summer drink. Adjust sugar content for desired tartness and add a fresh mint garnish, if you wish.

MINTED GINGER ALE

    $1/2$ cup lemon juice
    2 tablespoons chopped fresh mint leaves
    8 cups ginger ale
    Sprigs of mint leaves, optional

Stir together lemon juice and chopped mint. Set aside for 15 minutes, then strain. Place strained lemon juice in large pitcher and pour in ginger ale. Serve over ice. Garnish with mint leaves.

Klover Schafer
For Everything There is a Season, Vermont Lutheran Church, 150 Years of Faith, Fellowship and Food

SWAMP WATER

2 shots vodka

2 shots apricot brandy

12 ounces limeade, mixed according to directions

Mix vodka and brandy in a large Mason jar (quart size), add limeade and serve in pint Mason jars if available.

Bonnie Mansfield

From Our House to Your House: Recipes from the Madison Curling Club

Adjust portions, according to number of thirsty drinkers.

CHRISTMAS PERCOLATOR PUNCH

1 quart apple cider

1 pint cranberry juice

1 cup orange juice

$3/_4$ cup lemon juice

1 cup sugar

1 teaspoon whole allspice

1 teaspoon whole cloves

3 cinnamon sticks

Combine cider, cranberry juice, orange juice, and lemon juice in automatic percolator. Place sugar and spices in percolator basket. Allow to go through perk cycle. Serve hot. Yield: 16 ($^1/_2$ cup) servings.

I make a 30-cup coffee pot of this for Christmas and they drink it all.

Janet Harvey

A Table in the Wilderness, Western Koshkonong Lutheran Church

SOUPS & SALADS

SPICY TOMATO SOUP

Roux:

> $^2/_3$ cup butter
>
> 1 cup flour

Soup:

> 2 large garlic cloves, minced
>
> 2 cups onion, diced
>
> $^1/_3$ cup butter
>
> 2 cans (29 ounces each) tomato sauce
>
> 2 cans (28 ounces each) diced tomatoes
>
> $^1/_2$ cup honey
>
> 4 to 6 dashes Tabasco sauce
>
> 1 teaspoon black pepper
>
> 1 teaspoon chili powder
>
> 2 teaspoons basil
>
> 1 to 3 tablespoons dill weed, according to taste

For the roux, melt butter in small skillet. Add flour; stir constantly for 3 to 5 minutes. Set aside.

For the soup, sauté garlic and onion in butter in a 10- to 12-quart soup kettle until transparent. Add roux slowly. Whisk constantly and cook until medium thick and smooth. Add remaining ingredients. Simmer 30 minutes, stirring frequently. Makes about 6 quarts.

Janet Castle
For Everything There is a Season, Vermont Lutheran Church, 150 Years of Faith, Fellowship and Food

This recipe can be halved for smaller quantities. Also, this is a very thick, rich soup and it can be diluted with additional water, if desired.

CHILLED AVOCADO, LIME AND CILANTRO SOUP

> 2 ripe avocados
>
> 1 small mild onion, chopped
>
> 1 clove garlic, crushed
>
> 2 tablespoons cilantro, chopped
>
> 1 tablespoon fresh mint, chopped
>
> 2 tablespoons fresh lime juice
>
> 3 cups vegetable stock

1 tablespoon rice vinegar
1 tablespoon soy sauce
Salt and pepper

Garnish:
2 teaspoons lime juice
1 tablespoon cilantro, chopped
2 tablespoons sour cream or crème fraiche
Fine shreds of lime rind

Halve, pit, and scoop out the flesh from the avocados. Place in a blender or food processor with onion, garlic, cilantro, mint, lime juice, and approximately $1/2$ of the stock. Process until smooth. Add the remaining stock, rice wine vinegar, and soy sauce and blend again. Taste and adjust for seasoning, adding more lime juice or salt and pepper. Cover and chill.

For the lime-cream garnish, mix together lime juice, cilantro, and sour cream (or crème fraiche). Spoon into the soup just before serving and sprinkle with lime rind. Makes 4 servings.

Sheila Getman-Sherwin
Pleasant Fridge: Pleasant Ridge Waldorf School Community Cookbook

Best if eaten the same day.

LORI'S PUMPKIN CURRY SOUP
$1/2$ cup mushrooms, sliced
$1/2$ cup yellow onion, chopped
2 tablespoons butter
2 tablespoons flour
$1/2$ to 1 teaspoon curry powder
3 cups vegetable broth
1 can (15 ounces) solid pack pumpkin
1 can (12 ounces) evaporated milk
1 tablespoon honey
$1/2$ teaspoon salt
$1/4$ teaspoon pepper
$1/4$ teaspoon ground nutmeg
Fresh chives (optional)

In large saucepan, sauté mushrooms and onion in butter until tender. Stir in flour and curry powder until blended. Gradually add vegetable broth. Bring to boil.

Cook, stirring, for 2 minutes or until thickened. Add pumpkin, milk, honey, salt, pepper, and nutmeg. Heat through. Garnish with chives, if desired. Makes 7 servings.

Lori Karst
From Our House to Your House: Recipes from the Madison Curling Club

EASY CREAMY CAULIFLOWER SOUP

   4 cups chicken stock, or equivalent in bouillon cubes
   2 cups water
   1 medium head of cauliflower, washed and diced
   1 large potato, peeled and diced
   1 small onion, diced
   1 or 2 tablespoons olive oil or butter
   $^1/_2$ to 1 teaspoon salt
   Pepper to taste

Bring chicken stock and water to a simmer in 3-quart stockpot. Add cauliflower and potatoes. Cook until fork tender. Meanwhile, sauté diced onion in olive oil or melted butter. Once cauliflower and potato are cooked, stir in onion. Process in blender or food processor in batches until smooth and creamy. Add salt and pepper to taste. Makes 6 to 8 servings.

Sally Wood
The Wisconsin Gardener Cookbook 3

SPLIT PEA SAUSAGE SOUP

   1 pound smoked sausage or kielbasa
   1 pound dry split peas
   6 cups water
   1 cup carrots, chopped
   1 cup onion, chopped
   1 cup celery, chopped
   1 tablespoon minced fresh parsley
   1 teaspoon salt
   $^1/_2$ teaspoon pepper
   2 bay leaves

Cut sausage in half lengthwise and then into $^1/_4$-inch slices. Place in a Dutch oven. Add remaining ingredients. Bring to a boil. Reduce heat; cover and simmer for 1 $^1/_4$

to 1 $1/_2$ hours or until peas are tender. Remove bay leaves.

Joanne Erdmann
Recipes and Memories, Trinity Lutheran Church, Arkdale

CARROT LEEK SOUP

1 medium leek, thinly sliced and rinsed of all sandy residue
4 teaspoons butter
6 medium carrots, sliced
2 medium potatoes, peeled and cubed
3 cans (14 $1/_2$ ounces each) chicken broth
2 cups whole milk
$1/_8$ teaspoon freshly ground pepper
1 cup half and half
Salt to taste after cooking

In a large saucepan, sauté leek in butter until tender. Add carrots, potatoes, and broth. Bring to a boil. Reduce heat; cover and simmer until vegetables are tender. Cool to room temperature. Remove vegetables with a slotted spoon to a blender or food processor. Add enough cooking liquid to easily process until smooth. Return to pan. Stir in milk and pepper; heat through. Add half and half and salt, as needed. Continue to heat but do not simmer. Serve with a dollop of sour cream and dash of nutmeg. Makes 10 small or 6 large servings.

Virginia Finke Urness
For Everything There is a Season, Vermont Lutheran Church, 150 Years of Faith, Fellowship and Food

CHEESE 'N BRAT SOUP

1 cup celery, chopped
1 cup carrot, chopped
1 cup bell pepper, chopped
2 tablespoons vegetable oil
6 cups chicken broth
4 bratwurst, cut in $1/_2$-inch rounds
1 teaspoon salt, to taste
$1/_2$ teaspoon black pepper, to taste
1 tablespoon Worcestershire sauce
Tabasco sauce to taste

Hot sauce to taste

1 cup Monterey Jack cheese, shredded

2 tablespoons flour

1 bottle (12 ounces) lager beer

In a large soup pot, sauté the vegetables in oil until lightly browned. Add the chicken broth; bring to a boil, reduce heat, cover and simmer until carrots are almost tender, about 30 minutes. Add the bratwurst, salt, pepper, Worcestershire sauce, Tabasco sauce, and hot sauce. Stir together the cheese and flour; add to the simmering soup, whisking to distribute thoroughly. Increase heat and bring barely to a boil, stirring constantly. Add the lager beer. Bring barely to a boil again and reduce heat; simmer for 5 minutes. Makes 6 servings.

Mike LaMantia and Russ Zucker
Cooksville Lutheran Church Cookbook

Variations on this Wisconsin-themed soup include adding a cup of onions (and cutting back on the green pepper to $1/2$ cup); adding additional cheese (pepper jack is good); and using precooked, smoked brats for extra flavor. A can of green chilies can also be substituted for hot sauce.

BLONDE GAZPACHO

3 cucumbers, seeded and diced

2 large tomatoes, seeded and diced

1 green bell pepper, diced

1 red bell pepper, diced

1 yellow bell pepper, diced

6 cups chicken broth

3 cups sour cream

1 small bunch Italian parsley, chopped fine

Dash Tabasco sauce

$1/2$ teaspoon coarsely ground black pepper

Salt, if needed

Sunflower seeds for garnish

In a large nonmetallic bowl, combine cucumber, tomatoes, peppers, chicken broth, sour cream, Italian parsley, Tabasco sauce, black pepper, and salt. Mix well and chill. Garnish each serving with sunflower seeds. If soup is too thick, thin with additional chicken broth. For a thicker soup, puree half of the soup in a food processor or blender and combine with original mixture. Makes 16 servings.

The Collection II: Simple & Elegant Recipes, Attic Angel Association

MEATBALL SOUP

4 cups beef broth

1 pound ground chuck

1 egg

1 teaspoon salt

$1/4$ teaspoon black pepper

10 green onions with tops, cut into $1/2$-inch pieces

1 cup thinly sliced carrots

1 cup thinly sliced celery

$1/2$ small head of cabbage (1 pound), finely shredded

2 tomatoes, peeled and cut into eighths

$1/2$ cup raw white rice

1 bay leaf

1 teaspoon dried basil

2 to 3 tablespoons soy sauce

2 tablespoons chopped parsley

In large stockpot, heat broth to simmer. Meanwhile mix beef, egg, salt, and pepper. Shape into small balls and drop into hot broth. Add onions, carrots, celery, cabbage, tomatoes, rice, bay leaf, and basil. Cover and simmer 35 minutes, stirring occasionally. Discard bay leaf. Stir in soy sauce. Add parsley and serve.

The Collection II: Simple & Elegant Recipes, Attic Angel Association

CREAMY WILD RICE SOUP

6 tablespoons butter, melted

3 tablespoons chopped onion

$1/3$ cup flour

4 cups chicken broth

$1/2$ cup cooked, cubed ham (optional)

2 cups cooked rice (wild or half white and half wild)

$1/4$ cup finely grated carrots

3 tablespoons chopped pecans

$1/4$ teaspoon white pepper

1 cup half and half

Sauté onion in butter. Blend in flour and gradually add broth. Boil 1 minute, then add ham, cooked rice, carrots, nuts, and pepper. Blend in half and half and heat to serving temperature.

Carol Johnsrud
Castle Rock Lutheran Church Cookbook

Add sherry (1 or 2 tablespoons) to this soup for extra flavor.

MIDWEST CHOWDER

> 2 cups diced potatoes
> $1/2$ cup sliced carrots
> $1/2$ cup sliced celery
> $1/4$ cup chopped onions
> 1 teaspoon salt
> $1/4$ teaspoon pepper
> 2 cups boiling water

Combine ingredients and simmer together for 10 minutes. Do not drain. Set aside.

White Sauce:

> $1/4$ cup butter or margarine
> $1/4$ cup flour
> 2 cups milk
> 10 ounces shredded cheddar cheese
> 1 16-ounce can cream-style corn

For white sauce, combine butter, flour, and milk in a large saucepan or stockpot. Add cheese and stir until melted. Add cream-style corn and vegetable mixture (undrained). Heat through. Yield: 6 servings

Kathy Horton
The Catholic Communities of St. Andrew, Verona, and St. William, Paoli, Cookbook

Adjust seasonings to your liking; add hot sauce or red pepper flakes to spice it up.

FOND FOOD MEMORIES

Mary Christenson, Development Director, Pleasant Ridge Waldorf School
Pleasant Fridge: Pleasant Ridge Waldorf School Community Cookbook

COOKING TIPS

▶ Before rolling out cookies, put the dough in the fridge to chill.
▶ I like recipes with lots of different spices, something flavorful, complex, rich, and authentic.

My first cooking model was from my large family. We lived in a farming community in Rosemount, Minnesota, which is south of the river by the Twin Cities. My mother had seven brothers and a sister and they all lived in the area. Our lifestyle back then centered on holidays and family gatherings: Thanksgiving, weddings, baptisms. We had many picnics, and a big one on Labor Day weekend. Food and sharing food were at the heart of these celebrations, such as Fran's delicious cream puffs that were made for graduations. Our menus were in tune with the seasons. At that time, we ate meals that weren't expensive; simple foods that could serve plenty of hungry people and tasted good.

Living in an agricultural area gave a real rhythm to life. We watched the sweet corn grow, and saw peas drop off the backs of trucks as they drove through town. Kids would run after them, collecting the vines that fell off to bring home to shell and eat. People used to hunt and fish. We ate deep-fried smelt when it was in season and lots and lots of sunfish, dipped in milk and breadcrumbs and pan-fried. In the summer it seemed like every few weeks there was a project involving food. We made most things—homemade noodles to go with cabbage, jams and jellies, canned or frozen vegetables and fruit, pickles, and even sausage and headcheese. There were two grocery stores with fresh local meat. You knew everyone in town well—and all the farmers.

From living and growing up in Minnesota, I moved to San Francisco and was thrown into the multicultural milieu of the city. My first job was in the garment industry and my coworkers were Peruvian, Jewish, Cantonese, and Hispanic; sharing food was one of the ways we got to know each other. Through food I was introduced to all of these cultures; it was a doorway for me to meet people and gave me an immediate access to a way of life.

The kitchen is a very intimate place in the house, so you share with others at a level that you might not achieve in other settings. Potlucks are connected with cooking and what we eat and what this means to us. Everyone brings a dish, so you have an immediate story. Potlucks weave a community together. You connect over the recipe and learn more about each other as a result.

I like to buy cookbooks and read them. For me, cooking is my art. It's both grounding and creative. I don't want to short-circuit it by hurrying. Food is our first medicine, what we really need—part of preparing and eating it is developing a sense of place, and identifying and feeling connected with that place. In my family, four of us have made careers of food at different times, the other three have owned restaurants or catering businesses—we all have a love for food.

ORIENTAL CUCUMBER SALAD

2 tablespoons white wine vinegar
1 tablespoon reduced-sodium soy sauce
2 teaspoons olive oil
$^{1}/_{2}$ teaspoon dried parsley flakes
$^{1}/_{4}$ teaspoon sugar or Splenda
$^{1}/_{8}$ teaspoon ground ginger
1 medium cucumber, thinly sliced
2 red onion slices, quartered

In a small bowl, whisk the vinegar, soy sauce, oil, parsley, sugar, and ginger. In a serving bowl, combine cucumber and onion. Add dressing and toss gently to coat. Refrigerate until served. Makes 2 servings.

Helen Wentler
The Wisconsin Gardener Cookbook 3

IOWA FARM GIRL SALAD

1 head lettuce, chopped
1 head cauliflower, chopped
2 cups mayonnaise
1 medium onion (mild), chopped
1 pound of bacon, fried crisp and crumbled
$^{1}/_{2}$ cup Parmesan cheese
$^{1}/_{2}$ cup sugar

Place ingredients in a bowl in the order listed. Cover tightly and refrigerate overnight, or at least several hours. Ten minutes before serving, toss well. Yield: 8 servings.
    May be cut in half. It is good.

Mary Sweeney
The Catholic Communities of St. Andrew, Verona, and St. William, Paoli, Cookbook

---

GRÜNER BOHNENSALAT (GREEN BEAN SALAD)

1 $^{1}/_{2}$ pounds green beans
Salt and pepper to taste
$^{1}/_{2}$ cup olive oil
3 to 4 tablespoons vinegar
1 medium onion, sliced thin
2 tablespoons parsley
1 teaspoon dried or fresh tarragon, or 1 teaspoon chervil (optional)

Cook the beans with $^1/_2$ teaspoon salt and enough water to cover the beans. Boil until tender but crisp. Drain and put the beans in a salad bowl. Combine the salt, pepper, oil, vinegar, onion, parsley, and tarragon; pour over the beans and toss. Serve at room temperature.

To keep overnight, store covered in the refrigerator. Best when eaten freshly made and warm. Delicious when served without the herbs as well. Makes 4 to 6 servings.

Dina Speich
Old World Swiss Family Recipes, Monroe Swiss Singers

BLUE CHEESE SALAD

Salad:

> Romaine lettuce
> Craisins
> Toasted walnuts, sliced
> Blue cheese, crumbled
> Chopped grilled chicken (optional)

Dressing:

> $^1/_3$ cup apple cider vinegar
> 2 tablespoons Dijon mustard (coarse)
> 2 shallots, minced
> 2 cloves garlic, minced
> Salt and pepper
> $^2/_3$ cup maple syrup
> 1 cup salad oil

Toss salad in a large bowl. Blend dressing ingredients in a blender, adding oil slowly. Makes enough dressing for several salads. Top salad with dressing and serve.

Mary Christenson
Pleasant Fridge: Pleasant Ridge Waldorf School Community Cookbook

---

ROASTED SWEET POTATO SALAD WITH WARM CHUTNEY DRESSING

Salad:

> 4 medium-sized sweet potatoes, peeled and cut into 1-inch pieces
> 5 tablespoons olive oil
> 1 tablespoon finely chopped fresh rosemary
> 1 teaspoon salt, plus more as needed

1 teaspoon freshly ground black pepper, plus more as needed

$1/2$ teaspoon ground cumin

$1/2$ teaspoon ground ginger

1 cup raw green pumpkin seeds (also known as *pepitas*)

1 cup dried cranberries

1 cup chopped scallions (green and white parts)

1 cup julienned roasted red pepper

Dressing:

6 tablespoons balsamic vinegar

$1/3$ cup mango chutney

2 tablespoons Dijon chutney

2 tablespoons Dijon mustard

2 tablespoons honey

2 cloves garlic, minced

$1/4$ cup olive oil

For the salad, preheat oven to 425 degrees. In roasting pan, combine potatoes, 3 tablespoons oil, rosemary, salt, pepper, cumin, and ginger. Stir to combine. Bake to fork-tender, about 25 minutes. Meanwhile, toast pumpkin seeds in 2 tablespoons oil over medium heat. Transfer seeds to plate and season with salt and pepper. In a small bowl, combine cranberries, scallions, and red pepper. Set aside.

Combine all dressing ingredients, except for olive oil, in a small saucepan and heat. Remove from heat and whisk in olive oil.

To serve, assemble the salad by gently tossing the roasted potatoes with the red pepper mixture. Add enough dressing to coat and garnish with toasted pumpkin seeds. Serve with extra dressing on the side.

Margo Koerner
From Our House to Your House: Recipes from the Madison Curling Club

This makes enough dressing for at least two salads.

JICAMA COLESLAW

2 cups shredded cabbage

1 cup peeled, julienned jicama

1 medium apple, peach, or nectarine, peeled and chopped

$1/4$ cup red onion, chopped (about $1/2$ of a small onion)

3 tablespoons reduced-calorie mayonnaise or salad dressing

2 tablespoons snipped cilantro or parsley

1 tablespoon cider vinegar

1 ¹/₂ teaspoons sugar

Dash to ¹/₈ teaspoon ground red pepper

Purple kale (optional)

In large mixing bowl, combine cabbage, jicama, fruit, and red onion. In a small bowl, stir together mayonnaise, cilantro, vinegar, sugar, and ground red pepper. Pour dressing over cabbage mixture, tossing to combine. Cover and chill for 2 to 4 hours. Place in a salad bowl. If desired, garnish with kale. Makes 4 servings.

Carla Lynch

From Our House to Your House: Recipes from the Madison Curling Club

---

MARINATED MELON SALAD

¹/₂ ripe honeydew melon

¹/₂ ripe cantaloupe

Small bunch of green grapes (optional)

3 tablespoons honey

2 ¹/₂ tablespoons lime juice

2 ¹/₂ tablespoons orange juice

¹/₈ teaspoon ground ginger

¹/₄ teaspoon ground cardamom

1 teaspoon almond extract

Remove seeds from melons and peel. Slice each half into ¹/₄-inch slices. Arrange slices on a platter with raised edges, in a circular pattern, alternating with 5 slices cantaloupe, then 5 slices honeydew around the platter. If desired, fill center with green grapes.

In a bowl, combine remaining ingredients, mixing until honey is blended into liquid. Spoon over melon slices. Cover and chill up to 4 hours before serving.

Klover Schafer

For Everything There is a Season, Vermont Lutheran Church, 150 Years of Faith, Fellowship and Food

SUNBELT SALAD

$^1/_4$ cup lemon juice

3 tablespoons honey

$^1/_2$ teaspoon dry mustard

$^1/_2$ teaspoon poppy seeds

$^1/_4$ teaspoon salt

$^1/_2$ cup vegetable oil

8 cups torn mixed salad greens

3 oranges or 2 grapefruit, peeled, sectioned and drained

2 cups fresh strawberry halves or slices

$^1/_2$ large sweet red onion, sliced and separated into rings

$^1/_2$ cup slivered almonds, toasted (optional)

In a blender container, combine the lemon juice, honey, and seasonings; blend well. On low speed, continue blending while slowly adding oil. Chill to blend flavors.

In a large salad bowl, combine greens, fruit, and onions. Just before serving, toss with almonds and dressing. Makes 4 to 6 servings.

Barbara Pelton

The Catholic Communities of St. Andrew, Verona, and St. William, Paoli, Cookbook

Olive oil is a good choice for this salad dressing; mix and shake the ingredients in a jar.

WHAT'S IN A NAME?

The affection felt by the cookbook contributors for people and customs, especially those of a former time, can be seen in the following recipe titles:

- Grandpa Luond's Pound Cake
- Bill's Boffo Potatoes
- Great Aunt Gracie's Ham Balls
- Doc's Special Brownies
- Nana's Oatmeal Cake
- Iowa Farm Girl Salad
- Marty's Meat Roll
- Grandma Weezie's Taco Pie
- Gilma Gilbertson's Beet Pickles
- Pastor Bob's Breakfast Enchiladas
- Jim's Special Request Pot Roast
- Aunt Marcella Hoffland's Oatmeal Cookies
- Millie's Company Muffins
- Grandma Keller's Sugar and Oil Cookies
- Edith's Potato Doughnuts
- Barbara the Great's Devil's Food Cake
- Grandmother's Bohemian Easter Bread
- Bubbe's Split Pea With Trieflach Soup
- Grandma Felland's Watermelon Pickles
- Hot Milk Cake, In Memory of Great Grandma Rein

SECOND HELPING SALAD

$^1/_2$ cup fresh lemon juice

Salt, to taste

$^3/_4$ teaspoon cumin

2 tablespoons olive oil (optional)

4 scallions, thinly sliced, white parts only

1 English cucumber, peeled, seeded and thinly sliced

1 pint cherry tomatoes, halved

1 can (15 ounces) chickpeas, drained and rinsed

$^1/_2$ cup roughly chopped flat leaf parsley

$^1/_2$ cup roughly chopped mint

$^1/_2$ bag salad greens

$^1/_2$ bag prewashed baby spinach

In the bowl you'll serve the salad in, whisk together lemon juice, salt, cumin, and olive oil. Add scallions, cucumber, tomatoes, chickpeas, parsley, and mint. Toss to combine. Add salad greens and spinach. Toss to combine, taste, and adjust seasonings. Serve immediately.

Carla Lynch

From Our House to Your House: Recipes from the Madison Curling Club

Add shredded carrots and mango, thinly sliced grilled flank steak or chicken, or serve over bulgur. Depending on taste, reduce amount of mint and parsley; chop the herbs finely or blend the dressing in a food processor.

TOMATO, BASIL AND COUSCOUS SALAD

2 $^1/_4$ cups chicken stock

1 box (10 ounces) couscous

2 to 3 bunches chopped green onions

2 diced tomatoes

$^1/_3$ cup coarsely chopped fresh basil

$^1/_3$ cup olive oil

2 tablespoons balsamic vinegar

1 teaspoon salt

$^1/_2$ teaspoon black pepper

Bring stock to a boil in saucepan. Add couscous. Remove from heat and let stand 5 minutes. Transfer to a large bowl and fluff with a fork. Cool. Add vegetables and basil. Mix oil, vinegar, salt, and pepper; pour over couscous. Mix well. Makes 8 to 10 servings.

Pat Wehrley
The Catholic Communities of St. Andrew, Verona, and St. William, Paoli, Cookbook

Can be made ahead and stored in refrigerator. Bring to room temperature before serving.

CHICKEN SALAD

$1/_2$ cup low-fat mayonnaise
$1/_2$ cup sour cream
2 tablespoons lemon juice
4 cups chicken, cut up
$1/_2$ cup cut up celery
2 cups grapes, red, green or both, halved

Combine mayonnaise, sour cream, and lemon juice, mixing well. Stir in chicken and celery. Gently add grapes.

Violet Korth
Family and Friends Cuisine, 2006. A Collection of Favorite Recipes from the Family and Friends of Willerup United Methodist Church

ZUCCHINI TOSSED SALAD

1 head lettuce
1 small bunch romaine lettuce
$1/_4$ cup olive oil
2 medium zucchini, thinly sliced
1 cup sliced radishes
2 tablespoons red wine vinegar
1 small clove garlic, crushed

Tear greens into bite-size pieces. Put in a salad bowl, toss with oil. Add all remaining ingredients. Makes 6 to 8 servings.

Peggy Korth
Family and Friends Cuisine, 2006. A Collection of Favorite Recipes from the Family and Friends of Willerup United Methodist Church

ORANGE AND ROMAINE LETTUCE SALAD

Dressing:
- $1/4$ cup vegetable oil
- 2 tablespoons wine vinegar
- $3/4$ teaspoon salt
- $1/2$ teaspoon ground coriander
- $1/4$ teaspoon freshly ground black pepper

Salad:
- 3 medium navel oranges, peeled, white pith removed, and sliced
- $1/4$ cup thinly sliced red onion
- 6 cups romaine lettuce, bite-size pieces, washed and dried
- $1/2$ cup sliced black olives

Whisk vegetable oil, vinegar, salt, coriander, and pepper in small bowl to blend. Add sliced oranges and onion; marinate for 15 minutes.

In a salad bowl, toss romaine lettuce and olives together. Add orange and onion mixture to greens and mix to coat greens. Serve immediately. Makes 4 to 6 servings.

The Collection II: Simple & Elegant Recipes, Attic Angel Association

---

RASPBERRY POPPY SEED DRESSING

- $1/3$ cup raspberry vinegar
- $1/2$ teaspoon salt
- $1/2$ cup oil
- 1 teaspoon dry mustard
- $1/2$ cup sugar
- 1 to 2 teaspoons poppy seeds

Blend ingredients, except poppy seeds, in blender or food processor. Stir in poppy seeds. Serve on spinach greens with sliced fresh strawberries, fresh mushrooms, and toasted pecans or cashews, adding cubed chicken for a main salad.

Complements of Cambridge postal clerk
Family and Friends Cuisine, 2006. A Collection of Favorite Recipes from the Family and Friends of Willerup United Methodist Church

Reduce sugar, according to taste.

CHEESE TORTELLINI SALAD

Dressing:

$^3/_4$ cup olive oil

$^1/_4$ cup white wine vinegar

1 teaspoon Dijon mustard

2 teaspoons fresh lemon juice

$^1/_4$ teaspoon sugar

1 teaspoon salt

$^1/_4$ teaspoon Greek seasoning

$^1/_4$ teaspoon black pepper

Dash of cayenne pepper

Salad:

1 pound tri-colored cheese tortellini

1 can (14 ounces) sliced artichoke hearts, drained

1 cup sliced fresh mushrooms

1 cup sliced black olives

$^1/_2$ red bell pepper (about 1 cup), thinly sliced

1 tablespoon drained capers

1 pound peeled, cooked shrimp or 2 cups cubed, cooked chicken

To make the dressing, combine oil, vinegar, mustard, lemon juice, sugar, salt, Greek seasoning, black pepper, and cayenne pepper in small bowl. Set aside.

Cook tortellini in boiling water according to package directions until al dente and set aside. When cool, place in salad bowl and add artichoke hearts, mushrooms, olives, red bell pepper, capers, and shrimp or chicken. Pour dressing over salad and toss. Chill. Adjust seasoning before serving. Makes 8 servings.

The Collection II: Simple & Elegant Recipes, Attic Angel Association

JANEEN JOY BABLER, SWISS FOLK PAINTER

Janeen Joy Babler is an artist, trained in Switzerland, who specializes in a style of Swiss folk painting called Bauernmalerei (similar to Rosemaling). While studying in Switzerland in the late 1980s, she was staying with a woman named Mrs. Candinas in a village called Hunibach, in the canton (state) of Bern. One must understand that except for the few large cities in Switzerland, most of the country is very agrarian, and contentedly grazing Brown Swiss cows are common everywhere. Mrs. Candinas asked Janeen to pick young spring dandelions from the backyard of her home for a salad. After they enjoyed the tasty salad, Mrs. Candinas said to Janeen, "Now you know what it is like to be a cow."

MRS. CANDINAS'S DANDELION SALAD

1 pound young, tender dandelion greens
4 strips bacon
1 medium onion
1 tablespoon vinegar
$1/4$ teaspoon salt
$1/8$ teaspoon black pepper
1 tablespoon sugar
1 tablespoon water
2 teaspoons chopped fresh herbs
3 tablespoons oil

Wash and drain dandelion greens and cut into bite-size pieces. Put into a salad bowl. Fry and drain bacon slices, dice. Dice the onion and brown in the bacon drippings. Add vinegar, salt, pepper, sugar, water, chopped herbs, and oil to make a dressing. Pour over the greens and toss.

Janeen Joy Babler
Old World Swiss Family Recipes, Monroe Swiss Singers

YUMMY CROUTONS

Bread ends, cubed
Olive oil
Spices (such as garlic powder, cumin, and a bit of thyme)

On medium heat (careful, these burn easily) throw the bread in with some olive oil. The oil disappears quickly so have some more to add as needed. The bread shouldn't be swimming in oil but needs enough to not stick to pan and to hold the spices. Cook and stir to evenly coat bread. Throw on some spices or not, as your mood and family dictate. Cook until somewhat browned—blackened is OK, it just adds character. Then add to your soups or salads and enjoy. They keep for a while in the refrigerator if you have any leftovers.

Sarah Caldwell
Pleasant Fridge: Pleasant Ridge Waldorf School Community Cookbook

This is a great recipe for all those bread ends, leftover toast, etc.

TOO MANY DANG ZUCCHINI

Help is on the way for that annual surfeit of end-of-summer zucchini. You do not have to abandon them in unmarked packages at the post office. Instead try some of these recipes:

VEGETABLES & SIDE DISHES

GERMAN GREEN BEANS IN HOT BACON SAUCE

1 to 1 $^1/_2$ pounds tender young green beans
6 slices bacon
1 medium chopped onion
2 heaping tablespoons flour
2 tablespoons sugar
1 teaspoon salt
Dash of pepper
$^1/_2$ to $^2/_3$ cup water
4 tablespoons vinegar

Wash, diagonally slice, and cook green beans until tender but still bright green (do not overcook). As beans are cooking, fry bacon in skillet until crisp; crumble. Sauté onion in fat until golden. Blend in flour, sugar, and seasonings; cook over low heat while stirring until smooth and bubbling. Remove from heat to blend in water and vinegar. Bring to a boil, stirring constantly, and boil for 1 minute. Add pieces of bacon. Pour over thoroughly drained green beans and blend. Makes about 6 servings.

Bonnie Stern
A Table in the Wilderness, Western Koshkonong Lutheran Church

---

GARDEN GRATINEE

2 medium, unpeeled potatoes (14 ounces total)
1 $^1/_2$ cups thinly sliced red and yellow sweet peppers
4 small trombone squash, thinly sliced (or substitute 2 small
      yellow summer squash and 2 small green zucchini)
1 teaspoon oregano
$^1/_2$ teaspoon salt
1/8 teaspoon pepper
$^1/_2$ cup grated cheddar cheese
1 tablespoon butter

Pierce potatoes and cook in microwave until tender but firm. Cool slightly. Cut in thin slices. Place peppers in microwaveable bowl, cover and cook on high for about three minutes, until tender and crisp. Spray a two-quart baking dish with nonstick cooking spray. Layer half the potatoes, squash, sweet peppers, oregano, salt, pepper, and cheese. Repeat layers. Dot with butter. Cover dish with foil that has been sprayed with nonstick cooking spray. Bake at 375 degrees for 25 minutes or until squash is tender and crisp. Uncover and bake 10 minutes longer. Makes 6 servings.

Christine L. Klessig
The Wisconsin Gardener Cookbook 3

"FRAGRANT GREENS" STIR-FRY

    2 tablespoons oil
    10 ounces broccoli cut into small florets
    $1/_2$ pound French green beans, stem ends snapped off
    1 sweet onion, cut into $1/_2$-inch wedges
    8 ounces cabbage, shredded
    1 tablespoon soft brown sugar
    2 tablespoons lime juice
    $1/_4$ cup Thai basil, shredded

Add oil to wok or large skillet, coating sides. Stir-fry broccoli and beans for 3 to 4 minutes, until vegetables are bright green and tender. Add onion and cabbage; stir-fry until just softened. Combine brown sugar and lime juice (make sure to dissolve sugar). Add to wok or skillet with the basil. Toss and serve immediately. Yield: 3 to 4 servings.

This is a very versatile recipe. You can substitute lemon juice for lime juice, sweet basil for Thai basil, and many other vegetables to your taste. Leave basil whole until needed. Noodles cooked ahead of time can be stir-fried with the vegetables, but the lime juice/brown sugar mixture should be doubled or tripled in that case.

Nellie Bednarek
Cooksville Lutheran Church Cookbook

SWEET POTATO QUESADILLAS

    1 $1/_2$ cups chopped onion
    4 cloves garlic
    2 teaspoons cumin
    2 teaspoons chili powder
    6 cups shredded sweet potato (about 3 large)
    Salt and pepper
    $1/_2$ cup cilantro
    10 flour tortillas
    1 $1/_2$ cups sharp cheddar cheese, shredded

Sauté onion and garlic until soft. Add spices and sauté 1 minute. Add grated sweet potatoes. Cover and cook 10 minutes, stirring frequently to prevent sticking and burning. Add salt and pepper to taste. Add cilantro, if desired. Lay tortilla on a plate. Cover half with sweet potato mixture. Sprinkle with cheese and fold tortilla over filling. Heat skillet over medium heat. Add 1 to 2 teaspoons oil. Fry quesadillas, turning over when slightly brown. Serve hot with sour cream and salsa.

Kristina Gullion
Pleasant Fridge: Pleasant Ridge Waldorf School Community Cookbook

BROWNED PARSNIPS

4 large parsnips
$1/_2$ teaspoon salt
$1/_4$ cup flour or cornmeal
2 tablespoons butter

Pare parsnips and slice in half lengthwise. Cook with salt in a small amount of water until the parsnips are tender. Strip out center core if woody. Dip the slices in flour or cornmeal. Fry in butter until golden brown.

Evelyn Beyer
Cooksville Lutheran Church Cookbook

ROASTED ASPARAGUS WITH OLIVES AND TOMATOES

1 $1/_2$ to 2 pounds fresh asparagus
20 small, sweet, and ripe cherry tomatoes
1 good handful of pitted black olives
3 tablespoons olive oil
1 clove garlic, finely sliced
1 good handful of fresh basil
Salt and freshly ground black pepper
1 small pinch of dried red chili flakes

Preheat oven to 425 degrees. Trim the asparagus and peel, if necessary. Add the asparagus, tomatoes, and black olives to a mixing bowl. Drizzle in the olive oil. Add garlic, basil, salt, pepper, and chili flakes. Mix all the ingredients together and then place in a hot pan or roasting tray. Cook in preheated oven for about 10 to 12 minutes, turning two or three times. Makes 4 servings.

Lynda McAfee
From Our House to Your House: Recipes from the Madison Curling Club

COOKING MEMORY

Marge Wallner
Recipes and Memories, Trinity Lutheran Church, Arkdale

COOKING TIPS:

I'm a big vegetable eater and I'm careful not to overcook them. I just use a little water or steam them. I also go by color. Asparagus should be bright green, which you don't see in the stores so much anymore. I also check to make sure the stalks aren't too large and I check the ends to make sure nothing is shriveled, so they won't be tough.

I come from a family of 10, and went to work at age 14 as a cook and a maid to help them out. My mother didn't follow recipes; she just knew how to add a pinch of this and a pinch of that. A lot of people back then felt that recipes were for those who didn't know how to cook. With so many children, my mother was always looking for thrifty ways to feed us. We had oatmeal for breakfast every morning, and the cookies were usually oatmeal. My mother made bread as well. Back then store-bought bread was almost unheard of at our house and a real treat. Times have changed, of course, and now I treasure homemade bread, though I'm just starting to eat oatmeal again.

When I was young, we picked our own wild asparagus growing in patches alongside the roads around Whitewater and Palmyra. My mother tried to stretch our food, so she would cook the asparagus in just a little water and then add milk, butter, salt, and pepper. This is still my favorite way to eat it. The milk gives it an especially good flavor. Today, I'm active in our church and I help coordinate the big bake sale the second Friday in December. I round up the rollers, clippers, and packers and for two days we make *lefse* (over 600) and Norwegian cookies. We always sell out. At 84, I'm just as active as I was at 65!

DILLY MASHED POTATOES

6 medium russet potatoes
$1/2$ cup milk
8 ounces sour cream
2 tablespoons minced fresh dill, or 2 teaspoons dill weed
1 tablespoon dried minced onion
$3/4$ teaspoon seasoned salt

In a saucepan, cover potatoes with water. Cover and bring to a boil; cook 20 to 25 minutes, or until very tender. Drain well; mash with milk. Stir in remaining ingredients. Makes 6 to 8 servings.

Donna Haakenson
Cooksville Lutheran Church Cookbook

STEAMED LEMON BROCCOLI

    1 large bunch broccoli, cut into spears
    1 medium onion, halved and thinly sliced
    1 cup thinly sliced celery
    3 garlic cloves, minced
    3 tablespoons butter or margarine
    2 teaspoons grated lemon peel
    1 $1/2$ teaspoons lemon juice
    $1/2$ teaspoon salt
    $1/4$ teaspoon pepper

Put broccoli in a steamer basket over 1 inch of boiling water in a saucepan. Cover and steam 5 to 6 minutes or until crisp tender. Rinse in cold water; drain and set aside. In a skillet, sauté the onion, celery, and garlic in butter about 5 minutes. Add lemon peel and juice, salt if desired, pepper and broccoli; heat through. Makes 4 servings.

Marlene Ludolph
For Everything There is a Season, Vermont Lutheran Church, 150 Years of Faith, Fellowship and Food

ACORN SQUASH STUFFED WITH APPLES AND CRANBERRIES

    2 small acorn squash, cut in half
    1 tablespoon butter or margarine, melted
    $1/2$ teaspoon salt
    $1/2$ teaspoon cinnamon
    $1/2$ teaspoon allspice
    $1/3$ cup dried cranberries
    2 medium apples, cored and diced
    $1/3$ cup brown sugar

Preheat oven to 375 degrees. Clean seeds from squash. Arrange squash halves (cut side up) in 9-inch-square baking pan. Pour water in the pan about an inch deep. Set aside. In a medium bowl combine melted butter and remaining ingredients. Spoon apple mixture into squash. Cover pan with foil. Bake for 45 to 60 minutes or until squash is tender; serve in small individual bowls. Makes 4 servings.

Ellie Schemenauer
Family and Friends Cuisine, 2006. A Collection of Favorite Recipes From the Family and Friends of Willerup United Methodist Church

ZESTY CARROTS

    6 large carrots
    Minced onion, to taste
    2 tablespoons prepared horseradish
    2 tablespoons butter or margarine, melted
    $1/2$ cup mayonnaise
    1 teaspoon salt
    $1/4$ teaspoon pepper
    $1/4$ cup breadcrumbs
    Parmesan cheese, grated

Scrape and cut carrots lengthwise, very thin. Cook, covered, in about 1 inch of water for 6 to 8 minutes, until just tender. Drain, but reserve $1/4$ cup of liquid. Put drained carrots in baking dish. In a small bowl, combine onion, horseradish, butter, mayonnaise, salt and pepper, and the reserved liquid. Pour over the carrots and mix well. Top with breadcrumbs and grated cheese. Bake in preheated 375-degree oven for about 15 to 20 minutes. Makes 6 servings.

Anita Strobel
From Our House to Your House: Recipes from the Madison Curling Club

VEGETARIAN SCALLOPED POTATOES

    12 medium potatoes
    2 tablespoons olive oil
    5 tablespoons butter or margarine
    $1/4$ cup flour
    Salt and pepper
    2 $1/2$ cups milk

Cut the potatoes into thin slices. Put olive oil in the bottom of a 2-quart casserole dish or deep-dish cast iron pan. Put a layer of potatoes on the bottom, dot with small pieces of butter (or margarine), and sprinkle with flour. Add salt and pepper to taste. Continue creating layers until all ingredients have been used. Pour milk over all, making sure flour is moist. Cover and bake at 350 degrees for 1 hour.

Maureen Karlstad
Pleasant Fridge: Pleasant Ridge Waldorf School Community Cookbook

SWEET POTATOES TOPPED WITH BRANDY AND RAISINS

$1/_2$ cup seedless raisins
$1/_4$ cup brandy
4 medium sweet potatoes
$2/_3$ cup brown sugar
$1/_4$ cup margarine
2 tablespoons water
$1/_4$ teaspoon ground cinnamon

Mix raisins and brandy in small bowl. Let stand 20 to 30 minutes; drain raisins. Boil unpeeled, whole sweet potatoes uncovered until just tender, about 1 hour. Peel and slice into $1/_4$-inch slices. Layer sweet potatoes in 9-inch-square baking pan. Top with raisins. Mix brown sugar, margarine, water, and cinnamon in small saucepan. Heat to a boil. Pour over sweet potatoes. Bake at 350 degrees for 40 minutes, basting with pan juice occasionally.

Dee Witcraft
Recipes and Memories, Trinity Lutheran Church, Arkdale

S.T.O.P.

Squash
Tomatoes
Onion
Peppers
Butter
Salt and pepper
Parmesan cheese, grated

Take any amount of the squash, tomatoes, onions, and pepper and sauté in butter until tender. Season with salt and pepper. Sprinkle with cheese.

Roberta Whittier
Cooksville Lutheran Church Cookbook

BABY BEETS

    1 bunch small spring beets
    Sour cream, to taste
    Salt and pepper
    $1/_2$ teaspoon fresh lemon juice

Cut off beet leaves, but leave 1-inch stems and root ends. Steam beets until just tender; then cool in cold water. Cut off stems and slip off skins and roots. Cube cooked beets. Add sour cream to taste, salt and pepper as needed, and a little squeeze of lemon juice. Heat and serve. Makes 2 servings.

Anita Strobel
From Our House to Your House: Recipes from the Madison Curling Club

---

SQUASH CHEESE CASSEROLE

    2 medium to large butternut or acorn squash
    1 cup chopped onion
    2-3 cloves crushed garlic
    Salt, black pepper, cayenne pepper and hot sauce
    3 tablespoons butter
    1 cup mixed green and red peppers, chopped
    2 eggs, beaten
    1 cup buttermilk or yogurt
    1 cup crumbled feta cheese or more, to taste
    $1/_4$ cup sunflower seeds or chopped nuts for the topping

Cook and mash the squash. Sauté the onion and garlic, lightly salted, in butter. When the onion is translucent, add the chopped peppers. Sauté until peppers are just underdone. Beat eggs with buttermilk or yogurt. Crumble in the feta cheese. Combine everything with the squash and mix well. Add salt, black pepper, cayenne pepper, and hot sauce to taste. Spread into buttered casserole or baking pan. Top with seeds or nuts. Bake at 375 degrees, covered, for 25 minutes, then uncovered for 10 minutes. Makes 4 servings.

Ruth Kittleson
Pleasant Fridge: Pleasant Ridge Waldorf School Community Cookbook

---

POTATO-FENNEL GRATIN

    2 small fennel bulbs
    1 yellow onion, thinly sliced
    2 tablespoons good olive oil
    1 tablespoon unsalted butter
    2 pounds russet potatoes (4 large)
    2 cups plus 2 tablespoons heavy cream, divided
    2 $^1/_2$ cups grated Gruyère cheese ($^1/_2$ pound), divided
    1 teaspoon kosher salt
    $^1/_2$ teaspoon ground black pepper

Preheat oven to 350 degrees. Butter 10-cup baking dish. Remove the stalks from the fennel and cut the bulbs in half lengthwise. Remove the cores and thinly slice the bulbs crosswise, making 4 cups of sliced fennel. Sauté the fennel and onions in olive oil and butter on medium-low heat for 15 minutes until tender. Peel the potatoes; then thinly slice. Mix the sliced potatoes in a large bowl with 2 cups of cream, 2 cups of Gruyère, salt, and pepper. Add the sautéed fennel and onions; mix well. Pour into the baking dish. Press down to smooth. Combine the remaining 2 tablespoons of cream and $^1/_2$ cup of Gruyère and sprinkle on the top. Bake for 1 $^1/_2$ hours until the potatoes are very tender and the top is browned and bubbly. Set aside 10 minutes before serving.

Becky Reilly
Sharing Our Recipes: A Collection by the Park Elementary School PTA, Cross Plains

SWISS INDEPENDENCE POTLUCKS

Deborah Krauss Smith, director
Monroe Swiss Singers

Each year the Monroe Swiss Singers hold a celebration on August 1, which is Swiss Independence Day. Our annual event combines some elements of the Old and New Worlds. We have a huge potluck (New World) in our machine shed, inviting singers

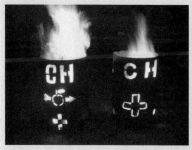

as well as others who are Swiss or of Swiss descent and enjoy celebrating the Old World holiday. Some of the foods are ethnic, such as *Kalberwurst* (in our recipe book), but it is mostly a really good American potluck. The Old World part is the informal accordion playing and singing, as well as the lighting of fires, which commemorate the signal used among the mountains in Switzerland in

1291 to announce that independence had been achieved. Some of our August 1 gatherings have had actual large bonfires, but we've also used burning barrels for a more contained fire. The "CH' on the barrels stands for *"Confederatia Helvetica,"* the Latin name for Switzerland and the European country abbreviation for Switzerland; the cross is from the Swiss flag; and the apple with the arrow through it is, of course, from the Swiss legend about Wilhelm Tell.

NOODLE KUGEL

8 ounce package egg noodles
8 ounce package cream cheese
$1/2$ pound butter, divided
4 eggs
1 $1/2$ cups milk
3 tablespoons sugar, divided

Cook noodles and drain, set aside. Blend cream cheese with half of the butter. Combine with eggs, milk, and half of the sugar. Mix with noodles. Melt the other half of butter in a 9-by-13-inch pan. Pour noodles in pan and bake at 350 degrees for 45 minutes or until brown.

Eleanor Frederick
Old World Swiss Family Recipes, Monroe Swiss Singers

VEGETABLE YORKSHIRE PUDDING

1 1/2 cups water, divided
2 cups broccoli florets
1 3/4 cups flour
1 cup milk
4 eggs
1 1/2 teaspoons salt
1/4 teaspoon pepper
1/3 cup butter
1/2 cup thin carrot strips, made by running peeler lengthwise on carrot

Preheat oven to 400 degrees. In 2-quart pan bring 1/2 cup water to a boil. Add broccoli and cook until crisp tender (about 2 to 3 minutes). Rinse in cold water. Drain. In large mixing bowl, combine flour, milk, 1 cup water, eggs, salt, and pepper. Beat on low until smooth (about 1 to 2 minutes). Meanwhile, in a 9-by-13-inch baking pan, melt butter in oven (about 3 minutes). Pour batter into hot baking pan; sprinkle broccoli and carrots over top. Bake at 400 degrees for 35 to 45 minutes or until edges are golden brown. Serve immediately. Makes 8 servings.

Klover Schafer
For Everything There is a Season, Vermont Lutheran Church, 150 Years of Faith, Fellowship and Food

---

ALMOND WILD RICE

5 1/2 cups chicken broth, divided
1 cup golden raisins
6 tablespoons butter, divided
1 cup uncooked wild rice
1 cup uncooked brown rice
1 cup sliced or slivered almonds
1/2 cup minced fresh parsley
1/4 teaspoon salt
1/4 teaspoon pepper

In a small saucepan, bring $1/2$ cup broth to a boil. Remove from heat, add raisins and set aside (do not drain). In a large saucepan, bring 3 cups of broth and 2 tablespoons of butter to a boil. Add wild rice; cover and simmer for 55 to 60 minutes or until the rice is tender (drain if necessary).

Meanwhile, in another saucepan, combine the brown rice, 2 tablespoons butter and remaining broth. Bring to a boil. Reduce heat; cover and simmer for 35 to 40 minutes or until rice is tender (drain if necessary). In a skillet, sauté the almonds in remaining butter until lightly browned. In a serving bowl, combine the wild rice, brown rice, raisin mixture, almonds, parsley, salt, and pepper. Makes 10 servings.

Cathy Rathermel
Recipes and Memories, Trinity Lutheran Church, Arkdale

ÄLPLER MACARONI (ALPINE MACARONI)

6 medium potatoes, peeled and cut into bite-size pieces
2 cups macaroni
Chopped onions, sautéed in butter
1 cup grated Swiss cheese
$1/4$ cup butter
Paprika
$1/2$ pint cream

Cook potato pieces in salted water with more water than usual for 8 to 10 minutes, then add 2 cups of macaroni and cook together until the macaroni is done. Pour into colander to drain. Spray a 9-by-13-inch baking dish with nonstick spray (or butter it). Add half of potato-macaroni mixture, then $1/2$ cup grated cheese (or as much as you like), then the rest of the potato mixture and another $1/2$ cup of cheese. Top with onion (as much as you like), sautéed in butter. Sprinkle with paprika. Pour cream over the top. Cover and bake in 350-degree oven for 20 to 30 minutes or until heated through.

Trudi Thomann
Old World Swiss Family Recipes, Monroe Swiss Singers

RUSSIAN CASSEROLE OR "FAKE PIEROGI"

Mashed potatoes
Lasagna noodles, cooked
Chopped onion
A good bit of butter, $\frac{1}{2}$ to $\frac{3}{4}$ stick
Grated cheese
Salt and pepper

Brown the butter in a skillet, add onions, and cook until brown. Put a layer of them on the bottom of a casserole pan. Layer noodles, potatoes, cheese, and onions for a couple of rounds. Bake at 350 degrees for 30 minutes.

This casserole is a yummy use for leftover potatoes, and a fine comfort dish.

Arwyn Wildingway
Pleasant Fridge: Pleasant Ridge Waldorf School Community Cookbook

MAIN DISHES

WHOOPS, I FORGOT ABOUT THE POTLUCK!

Though some of these recipes require a bit of refrigeration time, they are easy to assemble and are perfect for getting overworked and overscheduled potluck participants off the hook.

- Apple, Pecan, and Blue Cheese Dip, page 6
- Hip Paddlers, page 121
- Linguine and Artichokes, page 78
- Minted Ginger Ale, page 14
- Oriental Cucumber Salad, page 25
- Roasted Asparagus with Olives and Tomatoes, page 40
- Sunbelt Salad, page 30
- Tomato, Basil and Couscous Salad, page 31
- Cow Pies, page 118
- Kade's Favorite Pasta, page 77
- Linguine with Ham, page 71
- Orange and Romaine Lettuce Salad, page 33
- S.T.O.P., page 44
- Steamed Lemon Broccoli, page 42
- The Potluck Tofu, page 75

TRUDY'S BEEF BURGUNDY

1 $1/2$ to 2 pounds beef chuck, cut into cubes
$1/2$ cup Burgundy or other dry red wine
1 can beef consommé, undiluted
1 medium onion, chopped
$1/2$ teaspoon rosemary
Freshly ground black pepper
$1/2$ cup dry breadcrumbs
$1/4$ cup flour

Place meat in casserole with wine, consommé, onion, rosemary, and black pepper. Stir in breadcrumbs and flour. Cover and bake at 300 degrees for 3 hours. Serve over rice or noodles.

Myra Myklejord
A Table in the Wilderness, Western Koshkonong Lutheran Church

OVEN MEATBALLS

For the meatballs:
>1 $^1/_2$ pounds ground beef
>1 $^1/_2$ teaspoons salt
>3 tablespoons chopped onion
>$^3/_4$ cup uncooked oatmeal
>$^3/_4$ teaspoon pepper
>1 cup milk

For the sauce:
>1 cup ketchup
>3 tablespoons brown sugar
>3 tablespoons vinegar
>$^1/_2$ cup water

Mix meatball ingredients together and shape into walnut-size balls. Place in a baking dish that has a cover. Mix sauce ingredients and pour over meatballs. Bake, covered, at 350 degrees for 1 hour or until brown.

Karen Moy
Cooksville Lutheran Church Cookbook

BARBECUES FOR A CROWD

>5 pounds ground beef
>3 $^3/_4$ cups ketchup
>$^2/_3$ cup water
>7 tablespoons vinegar
>5 tablespoons brown sugar
>1 cup chopped onion
>2 $^1/_2$ cups chopped celery
>5 teaspoons dry mustard
>5 teaspoons salt
>Dash of pepper

Brown ground beef and drain. Add remaining ingredients and simmer until celery is tender. Serve with favorite rolls or buns.

Barbecue also does well in a Crock-Pot. Great for potlucks, buffets, and parties.

Dorothea Jurgensen
Sharing Our Recipes: A Collection by the Park Elementary School PTA, Cross Plains

POTLUCK AND COOKING OBSERVATIONS
Beth Weber, Unofficial Potluck Coordinator
Human Resources Department, Madison Metropolitan School District

COOKING TIP

▶ I still remember my seventh-grade home economics teacher, Mrs. Natalie Freeman, who told us a good tip when using eggs in recipes and combining ingredients. First break the eggs individually into a smaller container, like a custard cup, before adding them to the larger mixture. That way, if the egg is bad you won't spoil the rest of the batter. It's a great tip, and I have never seen any of the chefs on television doing this.

Our group has a potluck here once a month at least. If there's food, people will come. I think the importance of potlucks is the sharing, the food and the friendship. Just getting together over food brings people together. It's also a way to expand your own recipe base. Every year at work, I do a big Super Bowl spread and try to cook foods that reflect the regions of the competing teams. I read a lot of recipe books 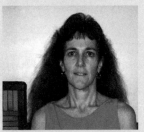 and what I like about community cookbooks are the handed-down recipes that you might not find anywhere else.

My Jewish grandparents were from Russia, so I grew up with noodle kugel, blintzes, and borscht with sour cream and hot potatoes. My grandmother's specialty was prunes with wine sauce. She used an old grape-jelly jar and filled it with pitted prunes, each stuffed with a half walnut and covered with sweet wine. This would set for several days. I really liked these as a child, and I realize now that part of this reason may be that the wine made me a little tipsy! My grandmother also made rugulah, a cream-cheese dough pastry with different fillings. It is time consuming to prepare, but I love to make it and eat it. It's my comfort food and links me to the past.

When we were growing up and my mother went back to work as a teacher, she still made a full meal every day with dessert. Everything was made from scratch, and there were very few convenience foods. Our food was always very colorful (borscht, tomato juice, grapefruit, etc.). Presentation was a big part of it—a sprig of mint on something made all the difference in the world. My mother even made leftovers exciting; she called them "katzy matzy." It had to do with being creative. You never knew what you would get. She taught me that you don't necessarily need a recipe; you just need to have confidence.

APPLE MEAT LOAF

  2 pounds ground chuck
  1 cup applesauce
  1 cup dry breadcrumbs
  $^1/_2$ cup ketchup
  1 teaspoon salt
  $^1/_2$ teaspoon sage

Combine beef, applesauce, and breadcrumbs. Add the ketchup, salt, and sage. Mix together well. Pack into a 9-inch loaf pan and bake at 350 degrees for 1 hour and 45 minutes.

Mary Hemesath

The Catholic Communities of St. Andrew, Verona, and St. William, Paoli, Cookbook

The applesauce keeps this light and moist. For a firmer loaf, use additional breadcrumbs. You can also play quite a bit with the spices.

BEWITCHING CHILI

  1 $^1/_2$ pounds ground beef
  $^1/_2$ cup chopped sweet red pepper
  $^1/_2$ cup chopped green pepper
  1 medium onion, chopped
  1 garlic clove, minced
  1 can (32 ounces) tomato juice
  1 can (15 $^1/_2$ ounces) hot chili beans
  1 can (14 $^1/_2$ ounce) diced tomatoes
  1 can (10 $^1/_2$ ounces) condensed beef broth
  1 can (6 ounces) tomato paste
  2 tablespoons chili powder
  1 $^1/_2$ teaspoons ground cumin
  1 teaspoon salt
  1 teaspoon sugar
  $^1/_4$ teaspoon pepper
  Sour cream
  Cheddar cheese

In a Dutch oven, cook beef, peppers, onion, and garlic over medium heat until meat is no longer pink; drain. Stir in tomato juice, beans, tomatoes, broth, tomato paste, and seasonings; do not drain or dilute any of the ingredients. Bring to a boil. Reduce heat; cover and simmer for 15 minutes. Garnish with sour cream and cheddar cheese, if desired. Makes 8 to 10 servings.

Alexia Gegare
Cooksville Lutheran Church Cookbook

HUNGARIAN GOULASH

$1/4$ cup shortening
2 pounds beef chuck or round, cut into 1-inch cubes
1 cup sliced onions
1 small clove garlic, minced
$3/4$ cup ketchup
2 tablespoons Worcestershire sauce
1 tablespoon brown sugar
2 teaspoons salt
2 teaspoons paprika
$1/2$ teaspoon dry mustard
Dash cayenne red pepper
$1 \, 3/4$ cups water, divided
2 tablespoons flour
3 cups hot cooked noodles

Melt shortening in large skillet; add beef, onion, and garlic. Cook and stir until meat is brown and onion tender. Stir in ketchup, Worcestershire sauce, sugar, salt, paprika, mustard, cayenne, and $1 \, 1/2$ cups water. Cover and simmer for 2 to $2 \, 1/2$ hours. Blend in flour and $1/4$ cup water; stir gradually into meat mixture. Heat to boiling, stirring constantly about 1 minute. Serve over noodles. Makes 6 to 8 servings.

Marlene Ludolph
For Everything There is a Season, Vermont Lutheran Church, 150 Years of Faith, Fellowship and Food

This goulash is good made with olive oil instead of shortening.

BEER BEEF STEW WITH DUMPLINGS

4 pounds lean beef cut into $1/2$ inch slices

$1/2$ cup flour

$1/2$ cup vegetable oil

2 pounds large onions, sliced

6 cloves garlic, crushed

3 tablespoons brown sugar

$1/4$ cup red wine vinegar, divided

$1/2$ cup chopped parsley

2 small bay leaves

2 teaspoons dried thyme

1 tablespoon salt

Fresh ground pepper

2 cans (10 $1/2$ ounces each) beef broth

24 ounces beer

2 cups all-purpose baking mix such as Bisquick

$2/3$ cup milk

Preheat oven to 325 degrees. Cut beef slices into 2-inch pieces. Dust with flour and brown a few at a time in the cooking oil. Place in a large ovenproof casserole. Add onions and garlic to oil in pan and brown them lightly, adding more oil if needed. Add to casserole along with brown sugar, 2 tablespoons of the vinegar, parsley, bay leaves, thyme, salt, and pepper. Pour off any oil remaining in the skillet. Add broth and heat over low heat, stirring to deglaze the pan. Pour over meat mixture. Add the beer. Cover casserole and bake for 2 hours. Transfer casserole to top of the stove. Stir in the remaining vinegar. Cook over medium high heat until sauce bubbles.

Stir baking mix and milk together until soft dough forms. Drop dumpling dough by spoonfuls onto boiling stew. Reduce heat to simmering, and cook uncovered for 10 minutes; cover and cook 10 minutes.

The Collection II: Simple & Elegant Recipes, Attic Angel Association

BRANDY MARINADE FOR BEEF

$1/2$ cup brandy

$1/2$ cup olive oil or vegetable oil

$1/4$ cup Worcestershire sauce

$1/4$ cup water

2 cloves garlic, minced

2 teaspoons sugar

2 bay leaves

$^1/_4$ teaspoon freshly ground black pepper

Combine brandy, oil, Worcestershire sauce, water, garlic, sugar, bay leaves, and black pepper in a non-corrosive container with a cover. When using, combine meat and marinade in a large heavy plastic bag, seal, rotate bag to coat meat, and place in a shallow baking dish. Refrigerate for 2 to 8 hours. If marinade is to be used for basting or as a sauce, place marinade in saucepan and vigorously boil for 3 minutes. Makes 2 cups.

During grilling season, make a double batch of this recipe, refrigerate and have available for quick easy grilling.

The Collection II: Simple & Elegant Recipes, Attic Angel Association

QUICK CASHEW CURRY CHICKEN

1 medium onion, chopped

1 to 2 cloves garlic, finely chopped

2 tablespoons butter

1 $^1/_2$ pounds chicken, cut into small cubes

1 $^1/_2$ teaspoons curry powder

1 tablespoon flour

1 $^1/_2$ cups milk

$^1/_2$ teaspoon salt

$^1/_8$ teaspoon cayenne pepper

$^1/_2$ cup chopped cashews

2 medium tomatoes, chopped

Sauté onion and garlic in butter; add chicken and brown. Blend in curry powder and flour, stirring constantly. Add milk and whisk until smooth; add the salt and cayenne pepper. Cook, stirring constantly, over medium heat until thickened. Add cashews and tomatoes; heat an additional 10 minutes or until meat is done. Serve over rice or broad egg noodles. Makes 4 servings.

Karen Knoll

The Catholic Communities of St. Andrew, Verona, and St. William, Paoli, Cookbook

CHINESE SOY-BRAISED CHICKEN THIGHS

4 cups water

$^3/_4$ cup soy sauce

$^1/_3$ cup sugar

$^1/_3$ cup balsamic vinegar or Chinese black vinegar

$^1/_4$ cup chopped, peeled ginger (fresh or the bottled kind found in
the produce section)

4 large cloves garlic, lightly mashed and peeled (fresh or the bottled
kind found in the produce section)

2 large whole star anise or 4 teaspoons star anise pieces or fennel seeds

3-inch stick of cinnamon

$^1/_4$ teaspoon red pepper flakes

Strained juice and half the rind of 1 medium orange

3 to 3 $^1/_2$ pounds boneless, skinless chicken thighs

Toasted sesame oil

Toasted sesame seeds

Chopped scallions or fresh cilantro

Combine water, soy sauce, sugar, vinegar, ginger, garlic, star anise, cinnamon, pepper flakes, and juice and rind in large pot and bring to a boil over high heat. Reduce heat and simmer, covered, for 5 minutes. Add the chicken to the pan and reduce heat so that the liquid barely bubbles. Cover and cook for 35 minutes. Remove from heat and let stand 30 to 60 minutes. Remove the chicken to a cutting board and brush liberally with toasted sesame oil. Arrange on a platter and sprinkle with toasted sesame seeds and chopped scallions or fresh cilantro.

When braised slowly in soy sauce, sugar, and spices, chicken takes on a beautiful deep brown color and an irresistible sweet-salty flavor. This dish can be served as a main course but is more commonly presented as an appetizer.

Cleo Ware
Castle Rock Lutheran Church Cookbook

ADRIANA T'S FAVORITE CHICKEN

2 tablespoons virgin olive oil

2 thick slices of onion

2 cloves of garlic, chopped

Juice of $^1/_2$ lemon, reserving some of the rind

Juice of $^1/_2$ lime, reserving some of the rind

2 chicken breasts, skinned, boned and cut lengthwise 1-inch thick
1 tablespoon fresh oregano, chopped
$1/2$ teaspoon seasoned salt
$1/2$ fresh ground black pepper

Heat skillet to medium heat. Add olive oil to heat and sauté onions and garlic, cooking until about halfway done. Add a few pieces (about 1-by-1 $1/2$-inches) of reserved lemon and lime peels and the chicken. Continue to sauté, adding the oregano, salt, and pepper.

When chicken is about three-quarters of the way done, add the lemon and lime juices and finish cooking. Remove chicken and serve. Adjust seasoning to taste. Goes great when served with steamed garden-fresh broccoli and onions alongside brown rice. Strained sauce from the sauté is delectable when drizzled over the rice. Makes 2 to 3 servings.

As we developed this recipe, my now 8-year-old daughter, Adriana, was just enamored with this concoction and I've never had to coax her to clean her plate. What else could we name it!

Brian J. Brickle
The Wisconsin Gardener Cookbook 3

CHICKEN PASTA TOSS

5 green onions, chopped
2 cloves garlic, minced
2 tablespoons butter
2 tablespoons olive oil
1 $1/2$ pounds chicken, cubed
3 tablespoons lemon juice
3 tablespoons parsley, minced
$1/2$ to $3/4$ teaspoon lemon pepper seasoning
8 ounces spiral pasta
Parmesan cheese

In a large skillet, sauté onions and garlic in butter and oil. Stir in chicken, lemon juice, parsley, and lemon pepper. Sauté for 15 to 20 minutes or until chicken juices run clear. Meanwhile, cook pasta and drain. Add to chicken in a large bowl and top with Parmesan cheese.

Lori Neumann
Sharing Our Recipes: A Collection by the Park Elementary School PTA, Cross Plains

CHICKEN IN PEANUT SAUCE

2 teaspoons minced garlic
2 teaspoons minced fresh gingerroot
1 teaspoon peanut oil
1 cup chicken broth
$^1/_2$ cup dry sherry
$^1/_3$ (heaping) cup peanut butter
2 teaspoons soy sauce
2 teaspoons rice wine vinegar
2 teaspoons sesame oil
Crushed red pepper flakes to taste
8 ounces cooked chicken breast
3 cups hot cooked vermicelli noodles
2 teaspoons scallions

Sauté garlic and gingerroot in peanut oil briefly. Add broth, sherry, peanut butter, soy sauce, vinegar, sesame oil, and red pepper flakes; bring to a boil and cook until smooth and thick. Add chicken. Serve over hot vermicelli and sprinkle with scallions.

From Our House to Your House: Recipes from the Madison Curling Club

CHICKEN ENCHILADA CASSEROLE

1 cup chopped onion
$^1/_2$ cup chopped green pepper
5 tablespoons butter or margarine, divided (2 tablespoons and 3 tablespoons)
2 cups chopped cooked chicken or turkey
1 small can green chili peppers, drained, seeded, and chopped
$^1/_4$ cup flour
1 teaspoon ground coriander seeds
$^3/_4$ teaspoon salt
2 $^1/_2$ cups chicken broth
1 cup sour cream
1 $^1/_2$ cups shredded Monterey Jack cheese
12 6-inch tortillas

In a large saucepan, cook onion and green pepper in 2 tablespoons butter until tender. Combine in a bowl along with chopped chicken and green chili peppers, set aside.

In the same pan, melt the 3 tablespoons butter. Blend in flour, coriander, and salt. Stir in chicken broth all at once and cook and stir until thick and bubbly. Remove from heat. Stir in sour cream and half cup of cheese. Separate half a cup of sauce from this mixture and stir it into the bowl with the chicken and peppers.

Dip each tortilla into remaining sauce to soften. Then fill each tortilla with about $1/4$ cup of the chicken/sauce mixture. Roll these up and place in a 9-by-13-inch baking pan that has been sprayed first with nonstick cooking spray. Arrange rolls to fill the pan and pour remaining sauce over the top. Sprinkle with the rest of the cheese. Bake uncovered in a 350-degree oven for about 25 minutes or until bubbly. Makes 6 servings.

Karla Freimuth
Sharing Our Recipes: A Collection by the Park Elementary School PTA, Cross Plains

---

TOMATO CURRY CHICKEN

4 skinless, boneless chicken breasts
2 tablespoons butter
1 onion, chopped
$2/3$ cup beer
1 can (10 $3/4$ ounces) condensed tomato soup
1 teaspoon curry powder
1 teaspoon dried basil
$1/2$ teaspoon black pepper
$1/4$ cup grated Parmesan cheese

Heat oven to 350 degrees. Place chicken in a 9-by-13-inch pan. Melt butter in a medium skillet over medium heat. Sauté onion, then stir in beer, soup, curry powder, basil, and pepper. Reduce heat to low and simmer about 10 minutes, then pour sauce evenly over the chicken. Bake for 1 hour, sprinkling with cheese for the last 10 minutes of baking.

Heather Pelzel
From Our House to Your House: Recipes from the Madison Curling Club

GRILLED CHICKEN AND PENNE

1 $1/2$ cups snipped cilantro

$1/2$ cup ricotta cheese

2 tablespoons minced garlic

2 tablespoons olive oil

$1/4$ teaspoon black pepper

2 teaspoons wine vinegar

1 teaspoon salt

1 pound cooked chicken

4 cups penne pasta

Place cilantro, cheese, garlic, oil, pepper, vinegar, and salt in blender or food processor. Process until well blended. Pour mixture over hot chicken. Serve with cooked pasta.

Roberta Whittier
Cooksville Lutheran Church Cookbook

CHICKEN-RICE EN CASSEROLE

$1/4$ cup or more chicken fat or butter

5 tablespoons flour

1 $1/2$ teaspoons salt

$1/8$ teaspoon pepper

1 cup chicken broth

1 $1/2$ cups milk

1 $1/2$ cups cooked wild or white rice

2 cups cut-up cooked chicken

$3/4$ cup sliced mushrooms

$1/3$ cup chopped green pepper

2 tablespoons chopped pimento

$1/4$ cup slivered almonds

Heat oven to 350 degrees. Melt fat in saucepan over low heat; then blend in flour, salt, and pepper. Cook over low heat until smooth and bubbly. Remove from heat, stir in chicken broth and milk. Bring to a boil for 1 minute, stirring constantly. Mix sauce with remaining ingredients. Put into greased baking dish. Bake 40 to 45 minutes. Makes 8 servings.

Grenneth Nelson
Recipes and Memories, Trinity Lutheran Church, Arkdale

CHICKEN ADOBO

1 chicken, cut up, or 5 pounds of thighs and legs, skinned if desired
10 cloves of garlic, peeled
10 peppercorns, crushed or whole
$^1/_2$ cup vinegar
$^1/_2$ cup tamari
Water or broth

Put chicken in a large saucepan with the other ingredients, adding water or broth so that the chicken is just covered. Bring to a boil, then simmer covered until tender, about 1 hour. Serve with soba noodles, garnished with chopped scallions, or with rice. Can also be served with mashed potatoes, especially if the gravy is thickened with a little cornstarch. Makes 6 servings.

This is a very satisfying dish because of the ingredients. My sister served this often in her bistro in Napa, California. It came from a recipe that a Chinese American co-worker showed me. The meat is so succulent it falls off the bone and it goes well with almost anything from Japanese Soba noodles to mashed potatoes.

Mary Christenson
Pleasant Fridge: Pleasant Ridge Waldorf School Community Cookbook

MUSTARD AND DILL FISH FILLETS

$^1/_4$ cup lemon juice concentrate
$^1/_4$ cup olive oil
2 tablespoons fresh dill
1 tablespoon Dijon or grainy mustard
1 clove garlic, minced
Salt and pepper to taste
1 pound fish fillets (sea bass, salmon, halibut or swordfish)

Whisk together the lemon juice, oil, dill, mustard, garlic, salt, and pepper. Pour mixture over fish and let stand 60 minutes. Grill over medium heat or bake at 375 degrees until done, 10 to 25 minutes.

Cleo Ware
Castle Rock Lutheran Church Cookbook

GRILLED SALMON ON A BED OF LENTILS

For the lentils:

    1 tablespoon olive oil

    1 small onion, finely chopped

    3 cloves garlic, finely minced

    1 cup lentils, washed

    2 cups chicken broth

    $1/_2$ teaspoon dried thyme or 1 teaspoon fresh

    $1/_2$ teaspoon freshly grated pepper

    $1/_2$ cup grated carrots

    $1/_4$ cup finely chopped fresh parsley

    Salt and pepper to taste

For the orange-lime salsa:

    3 medium oranges

    $1/_2$ small red onion, finely chopped

    1 small jalapeño pepper, finely chopped

    $1/_2$ cup finely chopped fresh parsley

    2 tablespoons fresh lime juice

    $1/_4$ teaspoon salt

    $1/_4$ teaspoon pepper

For the salmon:

    1 $1/_2$ pounds salmon fillets

    Salt and pepper

    1 to 2 tablespoons olive oil

    2 tablespoons Dijon mustard

    1 tablespoon lemon juice

    $1/_2$ teaspoon dried thyme or 1 teaspoon fresh

To prepare the lentils, in a medium saucepan heat the oil and add onions; cook until translucent. Add garlic and cook 1 minute but do not brown. Add lentils, chicken broth, thyme, and pepper. Bring to a boil, then reduce heat and simmer, partially covered, for 30 to 40 minutes or until lentils are soft. Add grated carrots and parsley. Cook 10 to 15 minutes or until carrots are tender. Add salt and pepper to taste.

To prepare the salsa, peel oranges and separate the sections. Remove and discard the membrane. Chop orange sections into small pieces. In a small bowl, combine oranges with the onion, jalapeño pepper, parsley, lime juice, salt, and pepper. Cover and refrigerate until ready to serve.

While lentils are cooking, sprinkle salmon with salt and pepper. In a small bowl, combine olive oil, mustard, lemon juice, and thyme. Brush mixture on salmon. Grill salmon over medium heat, turning only one time. Grill until lightly browned on the outside and completely done in the middle. Remove from grill and keep warm.

To serve, spoon lentils on serving plate and top with grilled salmon. Top salmon with orange-lime salsa.

Ellie Schemenauer

Family and Friends Cuisine, 2006. A Collection of Favorite Recipes from the Family and Friends of Willerup United Methodist Church

Salmon also can be fried in a small amount of oil over medium heat in a heavy nonstick skillet.

TOFU TUNA CASSEROLE

8 ounces tofu, cut into $1/2$-inch cubes
1 can (6 $1/2$ ounces) tuna, drained
$3/4$ cup mayonnaise
$1/4$ cup chopped onion
3 tablespoons lemon juice
$1/2$ cup grated American cheese
Dash of pepper
1 cup breadcrumbs

Heat oven to 350 degrees. Grease a 2-quart casserole. Cube tofu and drain on paper towel while preparing rest of ingredients. Combine tuna, mayonnaise, onion, lemon juice, cheese, and pepper in a large bowl. Fold in tofu gently to avoid crushing it. Spoon mixture into prepared casserole. Sprinkle surface with breadcrumbs. Bake uncovered 40 to 45 minutes or until nicely browned. Makes 4 to 6 servings.

Tofu makes this dish moist and delicious. It's a unique potluck item.

Sheila Grams

Pleasant Fridge: Pleasant Ridge Waldorf School Community Cookbook

TILAPIA WITH LEMON AND CAPERS

3 large lemons
1 cup flour
Salt and pepper
4 to 6 tilapia fillets
2 cups milk
6 tablespoons peanut oil
5 tablespoons unsalted butter
$1/4$ cup diced capers
2 tablespoons chopped parsley

Peel lemons, removing inner white membrane. Cut into segments and dice. Season flour with salt and pepper. Dip fillets in milk and coat with flour. Heat oil in large skillet. Sauté fillets on both sides for 4 to 5 minutes. Transfer to a serving dish to keep warm. Wipe out skillet; add butter and brown slightly. Stir in lemons, capers, and parsley. Serve over fish.

Cleo Ware
Castle Rock Lutheran Church Cookbook

EASY BAKED SHRIMP OR FISH

$1/4$ cup vegetable oil
1 pound shrimp, peeled and deveined OR
1 pound fish fillets cut into 1 $1/2$ inch pieces
1 tablespoon minced garlic
$1/2$ teaspoon salt
$1/4$ teaspoon fresh ground black pepper
$1/2$ cup Italian seasoned breadcrumbs
3 tablespoons chopped fresh parsley
Lemon wedges for garnish

Preheat oven to 475 degrees. Pour vegetable oil into a 9-by-13-inch baking dish. Add shrimp or fish. Sprinkle with garlic, salt, and pepper. Toss with breadcrumbs and parsley. Bake for 5 minutes, turn gently and bake for 3 to 5 additional minutes or until breadcrumbs are brown. Serve immediately with lemon wedges.

The Collection II: Simple & Elegant Recipes, Attic Angel Association

SHRIMP AND FENNEL WHAT YOU HAVE

2 tablespoons olive oil, plus a little more
1 large bulb fennel, cleaned and cut into $1/4$ inch slices
1 medium onion, coarsely chopped
1 rib celery, sliced
1 shallot, finely chopped
4 cloves garlic, halved
2 bay leaves
Salt and pepper to taste
1 cup white wine
Thyme sprigs or $1/4$ teaspoon dry thyme
1 pound shell on shrimp (20 to 26)
Fresh chopped parsley, to taste
1 to 2 tablespoons butter

In a 12-inch hot pan, add 2 tablespoons olive oil and the fennel, onion, and celery. Sauté until onions begin to turn clear. Add shallot, garlic, bay leaves, salt, and pepper; cook for 45 seconds. Do not brown. Add the wine and thyme; simmer until the fennel starts to get soft. Adjust the liquid to about 1 inch with wine or water and add the drained shrimp and chopped parsley. Stir and cover until shrimp are just cooked, about 1 minute. Add 1 to 2 tablespoons of butter and a dash of olive oil. Shake the pan until the butter melts. Adjust the seasoning and serve in hot bowls with a salad and crusty bread.

Lester Boles
From Our House to Your House: Recipes from the Madison Curling Club

REFLECTIONS

Lester Boles
Madison Curling Club

Food preparation has been one of my greatest pleasures for more than 40 years. My family taught me to appreciate roasted corn, country ham, and growing your own food. Outsiders, like Julia Child, taught me about the wonders of the culinary world, its people and cultures.

Dreams of preparing dinner for my family wake me in the morning, and the day unravels in the pursuit of fulfilling that dream. To my surprise, I never tire of performing cooking's most menial tasks. I love traditional cooking. It helps me feel grounded.

FARFALLE WITH WILD MUSHROOMS AND TOMATO SAUCE

4 tablespoons extra virgin olive oil, divided
$^1/_2$ pound sweet Italian sausages
$^1/_2$ pound wild mushrooms (such as hen of the woods), trimmed
        and coarsely chopped
1 medium yellow onion, peeled and chopped
3 cloves garlic, peeled and minced
3 pounds plum tomatoes, peeled, seeded and chopped
Salt and freshly ground black pepper
2 tablespoons finely chopped basil
2 tablespoons finely chopped fresh parsley
1 pound farfalle

Heat 2 tablespoons of the oil in a medium skillet over medium-high heat. Add sausages and cook, browning on all sides, for about 15 minutes. Remove sausages and cut into large pieces; set aside. Add mushrooms to skillet and sauté until golden, 1 to 2 minutes. Remove mushrooms from pan and set aside with sausage. Reduce heat to medium-low; add remaining 2 tablespoons oil and onions; cook, stirring occasionally, until onions are soft, about 20 minutes. Add garlic and cook for 2 minutes more. Increase heat to medium; add tomatoes and season with salt and pepper. Cook, stirring occasionally, until tomato juices have evaporated, about

15 minutes. Stir reserved sausage and mushrooms into sauce and cook for 10 minutes. Then add basil and parsley and season with salt and pepper. Meanwhile, cook farfalle in a large pot of boiling salted water until al dente, about 10 minutes. Then drain, toss with sauce, and serve.

Bonnie Kees
From Our House to Your House: Recipes from the Madison Curling Club

Omit the sausage and this could be a vegetarian main dish.

MAPLE BARBECUED PORK

    3 pounds pork spareribs
    1 cup maple syrup
    1 small onion, chopped
    1 tablespoon sesame seeds
    1 tablespoon white vinegar
    1 tablespoon Worcestershire sauce
    2 garlic cloves, minced
    $\frac{1}{2}$ teaspoon salt
    $\frac{1}{4}$ teaspoon ground mustard
    $\frac{1}{2}$ teaspoon ground ginger
    1/8 teaspoon pepper

Place ribs, meat side down, on a rack in a shallow baking pan. Bake at 350 degrees for 40 minutes. Drain and cool slightly. Meanwhile, combine the remaining ingredients in a saucepan. Cook and stir over medium heat until mixture comes to a boil. Cut ribs into serving size pieces; return to pan meat side up. Pour sauce over ribs. Bake, uncovered, for 1 hour or until tender.

Maxine Paxson
Family and Friends Cuisine, 2006. A Collection of Favorite Recipes from the Family and Friends of Willerup United Methodist Church

HONEY BARBECUE SHREDDED PORK

    1 $\frac{1}{4}$ cups ketchup
    1 cup chopped celery
    1 cup chopped onion
    $\frac{1}{2}$ cup water
    $\frac{1}{2}$ cup honey
    $\frac{1}{4}$ cup lemon juice

3 tablespoons white vinegar

3 tablespoons Worcestershire sauce

2 tablespoons dry mustard

1 teaspoon salt

$^1/_2$ teaspoon pepper

1 boneless pork shoulder roast, 3 to 4 pounds

Crusty rolls or flour tortillas

In a medium bowl, stir together the ketchup, celery, onion, water, honey, lemon juice, vinegar, Worcestershire sauce, mustard, salt, and pepper. Remove string or netting from pork, if present, and trim any fat from pork. Place roast in a 9-by-13-inch baking pan. Pour sauce mixture over pork and cover pan with foil. Bake at 300 degrees for 3 $^1/_2$ to 4 hours or until pork is very tender. Remove pork to a cutting board, reserving sauce. Using two forks, shred pork; place in a medium bowl. Skim fat from sauce. Add enough of the reserved sauce to moisten pork (about 1 cup). Serve pork on rolls or tortillas.

To cook this in a Crock-Pot, prepare the sauce mixture and meat as above. Place meat in a 4- to 6-quart Crock-Pot; pour sauce over meat. Cover and cook on low 13 to 14 hours or high 6 $^1/_2$ to 7 hours. Shred and serve as above.

Suzanne Hartley
Sharing Our Recipes: A Collection by the Park Elementary School PTA, Cross Plains

---

LINGUINE WITH HAM

1 package (6 ounces) plain or spinach linguine

1 cup sliced carrots

1 cup broccoli flowerets

1 cup sliced fresh mushroom

2 tablespoons butter

2 tablespoons flour

1 tablespoon snipped parsley

$^1/_2$ teaspoon dried basil

1 $^1/_4$ cups milk

1 $^1/_2$ cups ham, cut into cubes or strips

$^3/_4$ cup grated Parmesan cheese

Cook pasta and carrots for 7 minutes, stirring occasionally. Add broccoli. Return to boiling and cook 3 to 5 minutes more or until the pasta is tender-firm and vegetables are tender-crisp. Drain; keep warm.

Cook mushrooms in butter until tender. Add flour, parsley, and basil. Add milk. Cook and stir until thick and bubbly. Add ham and cheese. Pour sauce over pasta and vegetables. Toss to coat. Makes 4 servings.

Geri Despins
The Catholic Communities of St. Andrew, Verona, and St. William, Paoli, Cookbook

SPICED PORK TENDERLOINS

For the marinade:

5 bay leaves, crushed
1 teaspoon ground cloves
1 teaspoon ground nutmeg
1 teaspoon thyme
$^1/_2$ teaspoon allspice
$^1/_2$ teaspoon cinnamon
$^1/_2$ teaspoon basil
$^1/_2$ teaspoon pepper
$^1/_2$ teaspoon salt

For the tenderloins:

2 pork loins, 1 $^1/_2$ pounds each, trimmed
$^1/_2$ cup olive oil
$^3/_4$ cup maple syrup
$^1/_2$ cup Dijon mustard

Combine marinade ingredients. Brush tenderloins with oil. Rub marinade into oiled tenderloins. Marinate, covered, in refrigerator at least 3 hours. Bring to room temperature. Place in shallow roaster. Bake at 375 degrees for 1 hour.

Whisk syrup and Dijon mustard together. Heat in microwave. Slice tenderloin and serve with the mustard-syrup mixture in a bowl.

Connie McDonald
The Catholic Communities of St. Andrew, Verona, and St. William, Paoli, Cookbook

HOMEMADE PIZZA

For the dough:

2 $1/2$ cups flour

1 package instant yeast

$1/2$ teaspoon salt

2 tablespoons sugar

$1/4$ cup grated Parmesan cheese

$3/4$ cup hot water

1 tablespoon oil

For the topping:

8 ounces grated mozzarella cheese

$1/4$ cup olive oil

3 tablespoons red wine vinegar

2 teaspoons oregano

$1/2$ teaspoon red pepper flakes

1 tablespoon cornmeal

3 or 4 plum tomatoes, sliced

1 medium red onion, sliced crosswise in very thin slices

To prepare the dough, combine 2 cups of flour with the rest of the dry ingredients. Combine the hot water and oil and stir into the flour mixture. Turn out onto a floured surface and knead 8 to 10 minutes, using the remaining flour to keep from sticking. Place the dough in an oiled bowl, turning it so the top is oiled. Cover the bowl and set in a warm spot for 45 minutes.

If you have a pizza baking stone, place it in the oven and heat it to 450 degrees about 30 minutes before you want to bake the pizza. If you do not have a stone, preheat oven to 450 degrees.

While the dough is rising, marinate the cheese in a bowl with the oil, vinegar, oregano and pepper flakes for the topping. Sprinkle the cornmeal on a baking sheet. Pat the dough out to make a 14-inch circle, leaving the edge a little thicker. Spread the cheese mixture over the top. Make a circle around the edge of alternating slices of tomato and red onion. Make a second circle inside the first one in the same manner. Bake for 10 to 12 minutes.

Baking on a hot stone makes for a very crisp crust. Sprinkle a pizza paddle with cornmeal and form the dough on the paddle. Hold the paddle over the hot stone and jerk it back, depositing the pizza on the stone. Bake for 10 minutes.

Lynn Bednarek
Cooksville Lutheran Church Cookbook

TWO-SAUCE LASAGNA

1 tablespoon olive oil
3 cups sliced fresh mushrooms
$\frac{1}{2}$ cup chopped onion
2 cloves garlic, minced
9 lasagna noodles
2 cups shredded mozzarella cheese
1 container (15 ounces) ricotta cheese
$\frac{1}{2}$ cup plus 2 tablespoons grated Parmesan cheese, divided
1 small package frozen chopped spinach, thawed
1 $\frac{1}{2}$ teaspoons dried basil leaves
1 jar (14 ounces) spaghetti sauce (meatless)
1 jar alfredo sauce

Heat oven to 375 degrees. Heat oil in large skillet. Cook mushrooms, onion, and garlic in oil 8 to 10 minutes, stirring frequently. Drain. Meanwhile, cook lasagna noodles in a large pot as directed on package. In a large bowl, combine mozzarella, ricotta, and $\frac{1}{2}$ cup Parmesan cheese. In a smaller bowl, mix spinach and basil. In a 9-by-13-inch baking dish, spread 1 cup of spaghetti sauce. Layer with 3 lasagna noodles, a third of the cheese mixture, a third of the vegetable mixture, and the remaining spaghetti sauce. Top with 3 noodles, a third of the cheese mixture, a third of the vegetable mixture, and the spinach mixture. Top with 3 noodles, cheese mixture, vegetable mixture, and alfredo sauce. Sprinkle with remaining 2 tablespoons Parmesan cheese.

Cover and bake at 375 degrees for 30 minutes. Uncover and bake 15 to 20 minutes longer until hot and bubbly. Let stand 15 minutes before cutting.

Andrea Kendall

Family and Friends Cuisine, 2006. A Collection of Favorite Recipes from the Family and Friends of Willerup United Methodist Church

You may need large sizes (26 ounces) of both the meatless tomato-based spaghetti sauce and the alfredo sauce.

THE POTLUCK TOFU

Olive oil

Tamari

Spices—these can vary according to mood, family, etc. I prefer a
mixture of cumin, garlic and ginger, or alternatively, curry powder.

Firm tofu, sliced into squares, thin and flat

Sesame seeds

Put in oil enough to cover bottom of a pan. Dash in a fair amount of tamari and at least 1 teaspoon each of the spices. Stir this mixture and evenly distribute in pan. Lay tofu in and turn over to coat. On medium to low heat, begin to cook. Do not attempt to turn until sizzling sound indicates a kind of crispy effect. Turn over and do the other side. Tamari tends to evaporate quickly, so cooking slowly is best. Sprinkle with sesame seeds and serve.

Sarah Caldwell

Pleasant Fridge: Pleasant Ridge Waldorf School Community Cookbook

The size of the pan will depend on the amount of tofu you use. Also, for maximum flavor, use toasted sesame seeds.

MARINATED TOFU

Firm tofu

Olive oil

Tamari

Minced garlic

Spices

Veggies for stir-fry

Cooked basmati rice

Remove tofu from package, wrap in a clean dishtowel, and place in a colander with something heavy on top of it to press out extra liquid. Cut tofu into bite-size cubes. Place in a stainless steel mixing bowl and add enough oil and tamari to cover. Toss gently and let sit for 10 minutes. Place tofu on baking sheet and bake at 375 degrees for half an hour or until golden brown. Let tofu cool and set aside.

To prepare the stir-fry, fill wok or frying pan with 1 to 2 tablespoons of oil, 1 tablespoon (or more to taste) of tamari, and a good pinch or two of minced garlic. You also can add a pinch of cayenne, ginger, or five-spice if you wish. Sauté tofu and set aside. Sauté veggies until done, then combine with tofu and serve immediately over rice.

James Halberg
Pleasant Fridge: Pleasant Ridge Waldorf School Community Cookbook

---

MAKE-AHEAD SPINACH MANICOTTI

1 package frozen spinach, chopped
1 egg
1 teaspoon garlic
1 container (15 ounces) ricotta cheese
1 package mozzarella cheese, finely shredded
1 teaspoon Italian seasoning or to taste
$^1/_4$ teaspoon cumin or to taste
1 package manicotti noodles, uncooked
1 jar meatless spaghetti sauce

Defrost spinach and drain. Mix spinach, egg, garlic, ricotta cheese, $^1/_2$ package of mozzarella cheese, and seasoning in a bowl. Take noodles, uncooked, and stuff with the spinach-cheese mixture (using a ziplock bag with the corner cut off). Pour a little bit of sauce in bottom of 8-by-10-inch glass pan, place stuffed noodles on top of sauce and pour remaining sauce over noodles. Cover with foil. Place in refrigerator for at least 4 hours. When ready to bake, remove dish and let it warm up to room temperature. Then place in preheated, 350-degree oven for 30 to 45 minutes. During last 15 minutes, remove foil and place remaining mozzarella cheese on top.

Janelle & Delaney Osborne
Sharing Our Recipes: A Collection by the Park Elementary School PTA, Cross Plains

Although the recipe didn't specify, 2 cups of shredded mozzarella cheese and a 26-ounce jar of spaghetti sauce worked. For a stronger spinach flavor, use a large package of frozen spinach.

SUPPER CHEESE CASSEROLE

   8 slices bread, one day old
   Butter
   1 $^1/_2$ cups shredded cheese (any kind you like)
   $^1/_4$ cup green or red pepper, chopped
   $^1/_4$ cup onion, chopped
   3 eggs
   2 cups milk
   1 $^1/_2$ teaspoons salt

Preheat oven to 350 degrees and grease a cake pan. Butter the bread and fit 4 slices into the cake pan. Spread cheese and vegetables evenly over the bread. Cover with the other 4 slices, buttered side up. Beat eggs, add milk and salt; mix together and pour over the bread in the pan. Bake for 45 minutes or until golden brown.

Dee Draeger
Recipes and Memories, Trinity Lutheran Church, Arkdale

If meat is desired, add browned bacon or other cooked meat such as ham to the cheese-vegetable layer. Whole grain bread can be used as well.

KADE'S FAVORITE PASTA

   1 box penne pasta
   2 cloves garlic, minced
   1 small onion, chopped
   2 tablespoons olive oil
   1 can (28 ounces) chopped tomatoes
   $^1/_4$ cup fresh basil or 1 tablespoon dry basil
   $^1/_2$ teaspoon crushed red pepper flakes
   Salt and pepper to taste
   $^1/_2$ cup kalamata olives, sliced
   2 tablespoons red wine vinegar
   $^1/_2$ cup feta cheese, crumbled

Cook pasta according to directions on box. In a large pan sauté garlic and onion in olive oil for a few minutes. Add tomatoes, basil, crushed red pepper, salt, and pepper. Simmer for about 5 to 7 minutes. Remove from heat. Add kalamata olives and red wine vinegar. Spoon over pasta and top with feta cheese.

Julie Schultz
Sharing Our Recipes: A Collection by the Park Elementary School PTA, Cross Plains

---

LINGUINE AND ARTICHOKES
$^{1}/_{2}$ cup olive oil
4 tablespoons butter
2 teaspoons flour
1 $^{1}/_{2}$ cups stock
3 to 6 cloves garlic, crushed
2 tablespoons fresh parsley, chopped
4 tablespoons lemon juice
2 cans artichoke hearts
4 tablespoons Parmesan cheese, grated
2 tablespoons capers
1 pound linguine, cooked and drained

Heat oil and butter; add flour and stir. Add stock, garlic, parsley, and lemon juice. Cook over low heat for about 5 minutes. Add drained and quartered artichokes, Parmesan, and capers. Simmer for 10 minutes. Pour over pasta.

Cori Skolaski and David Heath
Pleasant Fridge: Pleasant Ridge Waldorf School Community Cookbook

COMFORT AND JOY

With the renewed popularity of slow cookers and regular family meals, the much-maligned casserole is making a comeback. Hosts are looking for comfort foods that would please the palate of a 4 year old as well as a 24 year old and a 44 year old—and an 84 year old and a 14 year old. With this in mind, the following comfort-food recipes are suggested:

- Chicken Enchilada Casserole, page 61
- Chicken-Rice en Casserole, page 63
- Honey Barbecue Shredded Pork, page 70
- Hungarian Goulash, page 56
- Meatball Soup, page 23
- Supper Cheese Casserole, page 77
- Tofu Tuna Casserole, page 66
- Trudy's Beef Burgundy, page 52
- Two-Sauce Lasagna, page 74

BREADS & BREAKFAST

BLUEBERRY BRUNCH BUNDT CAKE

1 cup margarine or butter, softened

2 cups sugar

2 eggs

1 cup sour cream

$\frac{1}{2}$ teaspoon vanilla

2 cups flour

1 teaspoon baking powder

$\frac{1}{4}$ teaspoon salt

2 cups fresh blueberries

Confectioners' sugar

Preheat oven to 350 degrees. Grease and flour a 9-inch Bundt pan. Cream margarine or butter and sugar in a large bowl with the mixer on medium speed until light and fluffy. Add eggs, one at a time, beating after each one. Blend in sour cream and vanilla. Combine flour, baking powder, and salt. Add dry ingredients to the creamed mixture. Gently fold in blueberries. Spoon the mixture into the Bundt pan. Bake 50 minutes to 1 hour. Remove to rack to cool. Dust with confectioners' sugar just before serving.

Dorie Underkofler
Cooksville Lutheran Church Cookbook

GUGELHOPF

1 cup butter

1 $\frac{1}{4}$ cup sugar

Juice and zest from 1 large lemon

3 eggs

$\frac{1}{2}$ cup white or golden raisins

3 teaspoons baking powder

$\frac{3}{4}$ cup milk

2 $\frac{1}{2}$ cups flour

Salt to taste

Combine butter, sugar, lemon rind, and juice. Cream well. Add eggs, one at a time. Mix in remaining ingredients. Bake in greased and floured Bundt pan at 350 degrees for 1 hour. Cool 15 minutes and remove from pan.

I remember this cake as a small girl; we usually had it on Sundays.

Marie Rufener
Old World Swiss Family Recipes, Monroe Swiss Singers

DOUGHCHIN

Dough:
1 ½ cups flour
¼ cup butter
1 teaspoon baking powder
½ cup sugar, more or less to taste
1 egg, beaten
Milk
3-4 cups fruit

Topping:
¼ cup butter
½ cup sugar
1 teaspoon salt
½ cup flour

For the dough, mix flour, butter, baking powder, and sugar. Combine beaten egg and enough milk to make 1 cup liquid. Incorporate liquid tenderly into flour mixture. Spread dough into greased 9-by-13-inch pan. Pour fruit over dough.

Mix together and crumble topping ingredients. Sprinkle over fruit. Bake at 350 degrees for 45 minutes.

Dawn Hundt
Pleasant Fridge: Pleasant Ridge Waldorf School Community Cookbook

CINNAMON SOUR CREAM COFFEECAKE

½ cup butter
1 cup granulated sugar
2 eggs
2 cups flour
1 teaspoon baking powder
½ teaspoon baking soda
1 container (8 ounces) sour cream
1 teaspoon almond extract
2 tablespoons brown sugar
1 teaspoon cinnamon
¼ cup chopped nuts

Cream butter and granulated sugar. Add eggs, flour, baking powder and soda, sour cream, and almond extract. Pour into an angel food or Bundt cake pan. Mix brown sugar, cinnamon, and nuts; sprinkle on cake batter. Bake at 350 degrees for 50 minutes.

Sandra Werthwein
Cooksville Lutheran Church Cookbook

RUM BUNDT CAKE

Cake:

> 4 eggs
> 1 ³/₄ cups sugar
> 1 tablespoon rum extract
> 1 teaspoon grated lemon zest
> 2 ¹/₂ cups flour
> 1 ³/₄ teaspoon baking powder
> ²/₃ cup milk
> ²/₃ cup butter, melted

Glaze:

> ¹/₃ cup sugar
> ²/₃ cup water
> ²/₃ cup rum

Preheat oven to 350 degrees. Grease and flour a 12-cup Bundt pan. In a large bowl, beat eggs, sugar, rum extract, and lemon zest until light and fluffy. Blend together flour and baking powder, then alternate adding the dry ingredients and the milk to the egg mixture, starting and ending with dry ingredients. Stir in butter. Pour batter into prepared pan and bake for 50 to 60 minutes or until a wooden pick inserted near center comes out clean. Cool in pan 10 to 15 minutes; turn out on serving plate.

For the glaze, in a saucepan, combine sugar and water and cook until sugar is dissolved. Cool and add rum. Pour glaze over cake. It may be served warm or cold.

The Collection II: Simple & Elegant Recipes, Attic Angel Association

Prepare the pan—vegetable oil spray or solid shortening works best—so it will release the cake without the aid of a knife, which could damage the cake's surface.

CRANBERRY POUND CAKE

2 cups sugar

1 cup butter, softened

5 eggs

$^1/_4$ cup sour cream

$^1/_4$ cup Triple Sec or Grand Marnier Liqueur

2 teaspoons vanilla

2 teaspoons grated orange zest

2 cups minus 1 tablespoon flour

$^1/_2$ teaspoon salt

1 $^1/_4$ cups chopped pecans

1 $^1/_2$ cups coarsely chopped cranberries

Preheat oven to 350 degrees. Grease and flour a 10-inch tube pan or a 9-cup Bundt pan. In a large bowl, with an electric mixer, cream sugar and butter until fluffy. Add eggs, one at a time, beating well after each addition. Beat in sour cream, liqueur, vanilla, and orange zest.

Blend together the flour and the salt. Add to creamed mixture, using low speed on mixer until just blended. Do not over-mix. Fold in nuts and cranberries. Pour batter into prepared pan and bake for 1 hour or until wooden pick inserted in center comes out clean.

Remove from oven and cool 10 minutes. Invert pan and cool completely before removing cake from pan. This cake is best if wrapped in plastic and left in the refrigerator for a day or so. When served, dust with confectioners' sugar.

The Collection II: Simple & Elegant Recipes, Attic Angel Association

This cake freezes well.

MULTI-GRAIN SCONES

Scones:

1 egg

$^1/_2$ cup sugar

5 tablespoons grapeseed or expeller-pressed canola oil

$^1/_4$ teaspoon lemon zest (or orange zest)

$^1/_2$ cup oatmeal (not instant)

$^1/_4$ cup wheat bran

1 $^1/_2$ cups unbleached white flour

2 tablespoons millet

2 tablespoons poppy seeds

$^1/_2$ teaspoon salt

1 tablespoon baking powder

$^1/_2$ teaspoon cinnamon

$^1/_2$ cup milk

Zesty lemon topping:

3 tablespoons freshly squeezed lemon juice (or orange juice)

$^1/_4$ cup powdered sugar

Preheat oven to 375 degrees. To prepare the scones, whisk the egg, sugar, and oil together in a bowl. Mix the lemon zest and all the dry ingredients together in a separate bowl and stir with a wooden spoon until all ingredients are evenly dispersed throughout. Slowly add the dry ingredients into the egg, sugar, and oil; mix to create a thick dough. Add the milk and mix well. Lightly grease a baking pan. Scoop up tablespoonfuls of the dough and drop them one by one in mounds onto the baking pan, leaving 2 inches of space between. You should have 10 scones. Bake for 15 to 20 minutes, just until the crust is barely golden brown and the dough is dry. Remove from the oven and let cool for 10 minutes.

To prepare the topping, mix the ingredients with a fork until sugar is completely melded in. Drizzle 1 tablespoon over each scone. Makes 10 scones.

Kris Loman
Sharing Our Recipes: A Collection by the Park Elementary School PTA, Cross Plains

RHUBARB BLUEBERRY MUFFINS

$^1/_4$ cup butter, softened

$^3/_4$ cup sugar

1 egg

$^1/_4$ cup sour cream

1 $^1/_2$ cups all-purpose flour

2 teaspoons baking powder

1 teaspoon salt

$^1/_3$ cup milk

1 cup fresh or frozen blueberries

1 cup chopped fresh or frozen rhubarb

In a small mixing bowl, cream butter and sugar. Add egg and sour cream; mix well. Combine the flour, baking powder, and salt; add to creamed mixture alternately with milk. Fold in blueberries and rhubarb. Fill 12 greased or paper-lined muffin cups about two-thirds full. Bake at 400 degrees for 20 to 25 minutes or until a toothpick comes out clean. Cool for 5 minutes before removing from pans to wire racks. Makes 1 dozen muffins.

Barb Wethal
Cooksville Lutheran Church Cookbook

For a tarter flavor, add an extra $^1/_2$ cup or more rhubarb.

CHERRY POPPY SEED MUFFINS

2 cups flour
$^3/_4$ cup sugar
1 tablespoon poppy seeds
1 tablespoon baking powder
$^1/_4$ teaspoon salt
1 cup milk
$^1/_4$ cup butter, melted
1 egg, slightly beaten
1 package tart dried cherries, about 1 cup
3 tablespoons grated orange zest

Preheat oven to 400 degrees. Grease a 12-cup muffin pan, or use paper liners. In a large bowl, combine the flour, sugar, poppy seeds, baking powder, and salt. Make a well in the center and add the milk, butter, and egg. Stir until just moistened. Gently stir in cherries and orange zest. Fill prepared muffin cups $^3/_4$ full with batter. Bake for 18-22 minutes or until light brown, and tops appear set. Remove to cooling rack and let cool in pan for 5 minutes. Serve warm.

The Collection II: Simple & Elegant Recipes, Attic Angel Association

STRAWBERRY MUFFINS

1 cup sugar
$^1/_2$ cup butter, softened
2 eggs
$^1/_4$ cup milk
1 teaspoon vanilla
2 cups flour
2 teaspoons baking powder
$^1/_2$ teaspoon salt
2 cups diced or chopped strawberries with 1 tablespoon sugar

Gradually add 1 cup sugar to butter and cream together. Mix in eggs, milk, and vanilla. Then add flour, baking powder, and salt. Toss strawberries with 1 tablespoon sugar. Fold berries into batter. Grease tins or use paper liners and fill two-thirds full. Sprinkle with sugar. Bake at 375 degrees for 25 minutes.

Evelyn Beyer
Cooksville Lutheran Church Cookbook

FAMILY DINNERS

Evelyn Beyer
Cooksville Lutheran Church Cookbook

COOKING TIPS

▶ I like to make roasts in a cast iron roaster; it heats evenly and the roasts come out tender and flavorful.

▶ The secret of great peach and cherry pies is to add a little cinnamon.

My mother was a fabulous cook, and as the youngest in my family, I grew up watching her in the kitchen, and later baking with her. All my Norwegian recipes are from her. She made wonderful cakes that she brought to church; and today I make rhubarb bread to hand out at our church to visitors, which comes from her original recipe. At home we always had big Sunday dinners with chicken and mashed potatoes and homemade noodles; this tradition has continued through the years and generations. I make the same things she did and the family still comes back to my house for fried chicken. My menu for Thanksgiving includes turkey and dressing; real mashed potatoes and gravy; squash; homemade noodles; cranberries; baked beans (not canned ones); and pumpkin pie, cherry pie, blueberry pie, and mincemeat pie. It is almost the same for Christmas, except my daughter does a duck recipe.

As foods become more mass produced, I have noticed the change in taste in meats, poultry, and fruits over the years. There is a tremendous difference in flavor between free-range and penned chickens, and you can see the difference in the color of the egg yolks as well. It's mostly in their diet. There's an old saying that has held true: "Chickens need to get out and scratch."

BLUEBERRY MUFFINS

$^1/_2$ cup oil
1 cup plain yogurt
1 egg
$^3/_4$ cup brown sugar
1 cup flour
1 cup oatmeal
1 teaspoon baking powder
$^1/_2$ teaspoon baking soda
1 teaspoon salt
1 cup blueberries

Mix oil, yogurt, and egg together in large bowl. In another bowl, mix brown sugar, flour, oatmeal, baking powder, baking soda, and salt. Add blueberries to dry ingredients and then add this mixture to the oil/yogurt/egg bowl. Bake at 400 degrees for 20 minutes.

Lana Stoddinger
Family and Friends Cuisine, 2006. A Collection of Favorite Recipes from the Family and Friends of Willerup United Methodist Church

You can use canola oil for this; you can also try different berries or a combination of berries, even rhubarb. These muffins do not rise much because of the yogurt and oatmeal but taste so good and are healthy.

APRICOT CRANBERRY BREAD

2 cups flour
1 cup sugar
1 $^1/_2$ teaspoons baking powder
$^1/_2$ teaspoon baking soda
$^1/_2$ teaspoon salt
1 egg
$^3/_4$ cup water
$^1/_4$ cup vegetable oil
2 teaspoons orange peel
1 cup cranberries
$^1/_4$ cup apricot preserves

In a large bowl, combine flour, sugar, baking powder, baking soda, and salt. In a small bowl, beat egg; stir in water, oil, and orange peel. Stir egg mixture into dry ingredients until moistened. Fold in cranberries. Pour into greased 9-by-5-inch pan. Spoon apricot preserves over batter; cut into batter. Bake at 350 degrees for 65 to 70 minutes.

Sheila Joethel
Castle Rock Lutheran Church Cookbook

RHUBARB BREAD

$3/4$ cup brown sugar
$1/3$ cup oil
$1/2$ cup buttermilk
$1/2$ teaspoon baking soda
$1/4$ teaspoon salt
1 egg
$1/2$ teaspoon vanilla
1 $1/4$ cups flour
1 cup diced rhubarb
$1/3$ cup granulated sugar
1 tablespoon butter, melted

Beat together brown sugar and oil. Combine buttermilk, baking soda, and salt; stir into the sugar mixture, then add egg and vanilla and beat well. Stir in flour and rhubarb. Pour into greased loaf pan. Combine granulated sugar and melted butter. Sprinkle on top of batter. Bake at 350 degrees for 45 minutes.

Evelyn Beyer
Cooksville Lutheran Church Cookbook

COOKING MEMORY FROM JEFF HORNEY
Award Winning Pie Baker

My grandmother, Lucy, was a Southerner, who was raised in Fredonia, Kentucky. Her rule for making cornbread or buttermilk pancakes was to whip buttermilk together with baking soda in a tin cup until the buttermilk "changes its tune." Folklore meets kitchen science.

STRAWBERRY-BANANA BREAD

3 cups flour

1 teaspoon baking soda

1 $\frac{1}{2}$ teaspoons cinnamon

$\frac{1}{2}$ teaspoon salt

$\frac{1}{4}$ teaspoon nutmeg

4 eggs, beaten

2 cups sugar

1 $\frac{1}{2}$ cups mashed strawberries

1 cup mashed bananas

1 cup oil

Sift flour, baking soda, cinnamon, salt, and nutmeg. Add remaining ingredients all at once. Stir until moist and pour into two 9-by-5-inch greased and floured pans. Bake at 350 degrees for 1 hour. Cool 10 minutes and remove from pans.

Mary Vroman

The Catholic Communities of St. Andrew, Verona, and St. William, Paoli, Cookbook

You can cut sugar to 1 $\frac{1}{2}$ cups.

LEMON BREAD

Bread:

$\frac{1}{4}$ pound butter, softened

1 cup sugar

3 egg yolks

1 cup sifted flour

1 teaspoon baking powder

$\frac{1}{4}$ teaspoon baking soda

2 tablespoons sour cream

Juice and grated rind of 1 large lemon

$\frac{1}{2}$ cup chopped nuts

3 egg whites, beaten until stiff

Glaze:

$\frac{1}{3}$ cup powdered sugar

3 tablespoons lemon juice

To prepare the bread, beat butter until foamy. Add sugar and egg yolks; beat well. Add flour, baking powder and soda, sour cream, lemon juice and rind; beat well. Fold in nuts and beaten egg whites. Pour into well-greased loaf pan. Bake at 350 degrees for 45 minutes.

For the glaze, combine powdered sugar and lemon juice. When baked bread is removed from oven, pour glaze over top.

Shela Fuller
From Our House to Your House: Recipes from the Madison Curling Club

For more flavor, add more lemon zest to the batter.

YOU ARE WHAT YOU EAT

Part of the great charm of community cookbooks is found by leafing through the index. You will often discover a full and fascinating spectrum of emotional characteristics and personality traits wedded to recipe titles. The indexes in the cookbooks used for Potluck! reveal these qualities and life situations:

CONFIDENCE
Out of This World Cookies
Truly Great Liver Pate
A Simply Good Salad Dressing
Fudge—The Best
Best Ever Banana Bread
Terrific Taco Salad
Super Star Pumpkin Bar
Unwaffling Waffle Recipe
Jytte's Fabulous Pie
Darn Good Chocolate Cake
Chicken Tremendous
Better Than Almost Anything Cake

PERSONALITY QUIRKS
Husband-Approved Lowfat Lasagna
Crabby Cake
Grandpa Hates Ketchup Meat Loaf
Not Yo Mama's Banana Pudding
I Told You So Lasagna

CULINARY OVERINDULGENCE
Pig Out Cake
Piggy Pudding
Heart Attack Potatoes

CREATIVITY AND IMAGINATION
Baby Food Cake
Grape Jelly Meat Balls
Avocado and Orange Floats
Salad Dressing Cake
Cherry Coke Salad
Lizard Pie
Everything But the Kitchen Sink Bars
Dreams—Scandinavian

SELF IMPROVEMENT
Must Be Good for You Popcorn

HARD WORK AND (SOMETIMES) HARD TIMES
Farmer's Suet Pudding
Hobo Stew
Poor Man's Cheese Torte

HUMOR
Rhubarb Do Funny
Smiling Pancakes
Swiss Chuckle

DESIRE
Melting Moments

SHYNESS AND LONELINESS
Blushing Apple Cake
Forgotten Cookies
Ugly Duckling Cake

ENTHUSIASM
Hoopla Chicken Lasagna
Inspiration Cake

AMAZEMENT
Surprise SB's Mashed Potatoes
Pinch Me Cake
Impossible Pumpkin Pie
Unbelievable Lemon Pie

SEASON PASSAGES
Touch of Spring Muffins
Daffodil Cake
Summer Flower Fairy Biscuits
Cold Weather Punch
Snow on the Mountain
Santa's Whisker's Cookies

LIFE CYCLES
Family Reunion Picnic Salad
Super Kid Energy Bars
Mints for Weddings and Showers

MODESTY
So-So Salad
Nothin Muffins
Old Stand By Hot Dish

AFFECTION
Friendship Tea
Mabel Hulsether's Big Softie Cookies
Thank You Torte
Friendship Tea
Good Old Mac and Cheese

AGGRESSION
Killer Baked Beans
Mucho Macho Nacho Popcorn

MULTITASKING
Self-Layering Salad
One Minute Fudge Frosting
Breakfast in a Cookie
Edible Peanut Butter Playdough
Time to Spare Ribs
In A Hurry Chicken Casserole

Several recipes seem to be perfect for the title of a book or a song, and beg to have a story or musical developed around them, such as Tea Time Tassies, Dark Secret (a dessert, of course), Chicken in a Cloud, Shooting Star Farm Autumn Stew, Mrs. Hon's Quick Buns, White Trash, Sally Ann, John Massetti, Leona Yelinek's Birthday Club Salad, and Frickadeller, which, of course, could be easily envisioned as a musical.

HOT SIN APPLE BREAD

Bread:

>3 eggs
>2 cups sugar
>1 cup vegetable oil
>1 teaspoon vanilla
>1 teaspoon baking soda
>1 teaspoon salt
>4 cups grated apples
>3 cups flour

Topping:

>$^1/_2$ cup sugar
>1 tablespoon cinnamon
>2 teaspoons flour
>$^1/_4$ cup butter or margarine

To prepare the bread, mix eggs, sugar, oil, vanilla, baking soda, and salt. Add grated apples and flour; mix together.

Combine topping ingredients and place half into the bottom of two loaf pans. Pour in bread batter; then sprinkle with remaining topping. Bake at 350 degrees for 1 hour. Remove from oven and let stand until cool before slicing.

Barb Luettgerodt
United Presbyterian Church 150th Anniversary Cookbook

Rhubarb can be substituted for the apples.

SPICY TOMATO BREAD

>2 $^1/_2$ cups flour
>1 tablespoon baking powder
>$^3/_4$ teaspoon salt
>1 teaspoon oregano
>1 tablespoon sugar
>$^1/_2$ cup grated cheese such as Asiago
>$^1/_4$ cup grated Parmesan cheese
>Milk

1 can (16 ounces) stewed tomatoes, drained, with liquid reserved,
    coarsely chopped

2 eggs

$^1/_4$ cup vegetable oil

Stir together flour, baking powder, salt, oregano, sugar, and cheeses. Add enough milk to reserved tomato juice to make $^2/_3$ cup. To that mixture, add eggs and oil, stirring to blend well; combine with flour mixture. Fold in chopped tomatoes. Batter will be thick. Bake in greased 8-by-4-inch loaf pan at 350 degrees for 1 hour or until toothpick comes out clean.

Jan Johnson

A Table in the Wilderness, Western Koshkonong Lutheran Church

Variations include adding basil, jalapeño pepper, or sun-dried tomatoes. This bread is very dense and would make a good appetizer or complement to egg-based brunch dishes.

FRESH HERB BISCUITS

1 $^3/_4$ cups flour

1 scant tablespoon baking powder

$^1/_2$ teaspoon salt

4 tablespoons cold butter, cut in pieces

2 to 3 tablespoons minced fresh herbs

$^3/_4$ cup milk

Preheat oven to 425 degrees. Whisk flour, baking powder and salt in bowl. Cut in butter until size of sunflower seeds. (Alternately, mix dry ingredients in food processor, cut in butter using machine, then dump mixture into separate bowl.) Sprinkle herbs over flour mixture. Pour in milk and stir briefly, just until a sticky dough forms. Turn onto floured surface. Knead lightly and briefly, four to six turns. Roll or pat to a thickness of 1 inch. Cut into rounds with floured biscuit cutter. Gather dough scraps and cut again. Place on ungreased baking sheet. Bake until high and golden, 11 to 13 minutes. Makes 6 large biscuits.

Bonnie Kees

From Our House to Your House: Recipes from the Madison Curling Club

BAKING NOW AND THEN

Bonnie Kees
From Our House to Your House: Recipes from the Madison Curling Club

Baking has held my interest for as long as I can remember. This interest may have evolved from my grandparents, who ran Back's Home Bakery for years at 316 East Main Street in downtown Madison. They operated this bakery until the late 1940s,  and afterward continued to bake breads, coffeecakes, and wonderful chocolate donuts in their home. One of my favorite recipes is their fresh herb biscuits. I use cookie cutters and place these biscuits on the top of a casserole while it bakes. I've used other biscuit recipes but these hold up the best, no matter how long they bake.

I also experiment with recipes by adjusting them to improve the nutritional value. I look for ways to trim calories by using less of an ingredient and lower-fat alternatives, especially low-fat cheeses or non-fat ricotta and substituting apple butter or applesauce in place of vegetable oil. I often add an extra ingredient to increase fiber, use smaller meat portions so it is part of the meal rather than the entire main meal, and add additional spices. I usually note on the recipe what did and did not work and substitute or adjust this the next time. There are always ample opportunities to bring in a dish to share at the Madison Curling Club potlucks.

FLOUR TORTILLAS

    2 cups flour, white or whole wheat
    $1/2$ teaspoon salt
    $1/2$ teaspoon baking powder
    $1/4$ cup oil
    $1/2$ cup warm water
    Extra flour for rolling out the tortillas

Mix together the flour, salt, baking powder, oil, and warm water until the dough forms. Knead the dough until it is smooth, about 2 to 3 minutes. Dough should not be sticky. Divide dough into 12 parts. Form each part into a flat, round piece about 1 $1/2$ inches in diameter. Let the pieces sit for about 5 minutes to make them easier to roll out. Using a rolling pin and enough flour to keep the dough from sticking (on the rolling pin as well as on the dough), roll the pieces into tortillas about 6 to 7 inches in diameter. Cook the tortillas on a hot, dry cast iron skillet, lightly browning them on each side. Eat while still warm.

Maureen Karlstad
Pleasant Fridge: Pleasant Ridge Waldorf School Community Cookbook

---

ORANGE GLAZED ROLLS

Rolls:
>1 package dry yeast
>$1/4$ cup warm water
>1 cup sugar, divided
>1 teaspoon salt
>2 eggs
>$1/2$ cup sour cream
>$1/2$ cup butter, melted, divided
>3 $1/2$ cups flour
>2 tablespoons orange zest

Glaze:
>$3/4$ cup sugar
>2 tablespoons orange juice
>$1/2$ cup sour cream
>$1/2$ cup butter, melted

Dissolve yeast in the warm water. Mix together $1/4$ cup sugar, salt, eggs, sour cream, and 6 tablespoons of the melted butter. Add the yeast and mix. Add 2 cups of the flour; beat. Beat in remaining 1 $1/2$ cups flour. Let rise until double. Knead 15 times on a floured board. Roll out half of the dough into a circle. Combine the remaining $3/4$ cup sugar and the orange zest. Brush dough with 1 tablespoon melted butter. Sprinkle half of the sugar-orange zest mixture over it. Cut into 12 wedges. Roll the wedges, starting with the wide end. Repeat with the other half of the dough. Place point down in three rows in a greased 9-by-13-inch baking pan. Cover and let rise 1 hour. Bake at 350 degrees for 20 minutes.

Combine glaze ingredients; boil 3 minutes, stirring constantly. Pour over rolls when still warm from the oven. Makes 24 servings.

Jeanette Retzlaff
Family and Friends Cuisine, 2006. A Collection of Favorite Recipes from the Family and Friends of Willerup United Methodist Church

INSPIRATIONS

Jeanette Retzlaff
Family and Friends Cuisine, 2006. A Collection of Favorite Recipes from
the Family and Friends of Willerup United Methodist Church

COOKING TIP

▶ When making dough for yeast breads, the water should feel like baby formula: warm but not too hot. If it's too hot it will kill off the yeast, and your rolls can turn out like hockey pucks.

My mother was a great cooking inspiration for me. She always made breads at home, along with rolls and cakes. The Orange Glazed Rolls recipe comes from her. She was a cook for a wealthy family in Chicago before she married my dad. Her specialty was fried chicken with really simple seasoning: salt, pepper, and paprika. We lived on a farm and got all our meat and eggs from it. It was a great shock to me later on to have to buy eggs and milk at a grocery store. A lot of good cooking starts with the question, "What do I have in the house right now?"

OVERNITE BUNS

4 cups water
1 ½ cups sugar
1 cup cooking oil
3 eggs, beaten
1 teaspoon salt
1 package dry yeast, dissolved in ½ cup water
12 cups flour

Boil 4 cups water and sugar for 5 minutes; cool. Add oil to sugar-water. Add eggs, salt, and yeast to the mixture. Add about 12 cups flour. Mix the dough around 2 p.m. and let rise until 5 p.m. Punch dough down well and let it rise again. About 9:30 p.m., shape into buns. Place on greased cookie sheets. Leave at room temperature overnight, covered with a dishtowel. Bake in morning at 375 degrees for 10 to 12 minutes. Makes 4 dozen buns.

Jeanette Retzlaff
Family and Friends Cuisine, 2006. A Collection of Favorite Recipes from the
Family and Friends of Willerup United Methodist Church

SOUR CREAM TWISTS

1 cup sour cream

3 tablespoons granulated sugar

2 tablespoons shortening

$1/8$ teaspoon baking soda

1 teaspoon salt

1 package yeast, dissolved in $1/3$ cup warm water

1 large egg

3 to 4 cups flour

1 scant teaspoon ground cardamom (optional)

1 tablespoon butter, softened

1 cup brown sugar

1 tablespoon cinnamon

Boil sour cream 1 minute. Stir in granulated sugar, shortening, baking soda, and salt. Cool. Add dissolved yeast mixture to sour cream mixture. Stir in egg. Stir in flour and cardamom. Knead dough 20 times. Cover and let rise 20 minutes. Roll out on floured surface to 24-by-6-inch rectangle. Spread with soft butter. Sprinkle with brown sugar and cinnamon. Fold top half over. Cut in 1-inch strips and twist. Place on greased cookie sheets. Cover and let rise 1 hour. Bake at 350 degrees for 12 to 15 minutes or until lightly browned. Frost while warm with powdered sugar frosting. Makes 26 to 28 twists.

Martha Peterson (submitted by Sharon Stoney)
Castle Rock Lutheran Church Cookbook

HARVEST BREAD

$1/2$ cup cornmeal

$1/2$ cup honey

$1/4$ cup oil

1 tablespoon salt

2 cups boiling water

2 tablespoons yeast

$1/2$ cup warm water

1 cup rye flour

4 cups whole wheat flour

1 cup toasted sunflower seeds

$1/4$ cup poppy seeds

Mix together cornmeal, honey, oil, and salt. Pour boiling water over this mixture; let stand to cool. Dissolve yeast in $1/2$ cup warm water and add to the cooled mixture. Add the rye flour and 1 cup of the whole wheat flour; beat well. Add the sunflower and poppy seeds, mix well. Stir in remaining 3 cups whole wheat flour. Let rise; punch down and divide into 2 loaves. Let rise until almost double. Bake at 350 degrees for 45 minutes.

Kristy Wiltrout
Pleasant Fridge: Pleasant Ridge Waldorf School Community Cookbook

BREAD IN A BAG

2 cups white flour
1 package yeast
3 tablespoons sugar
3 tablespoons dry milk
1 teaspoon salt
1 cup hot tap water
3 tablespoons oil
1 cup whole wheat flour

Put 1 cup of the white flour, the yeast, sugar, dry milk, and salt in a large zipper seal bag; seal and shake to mix. Add water and oil; close bag and squeeze until well mixed. Add 1 cup whole wheat flour and remaining 1 cup white flour; close bag and squeeze to mix again. Dough should not stick to bag. Knead bag 2 to 4 minutes. Let rest 10 minutes. Remove dough from bag and shape into a loaf. Place in a greased loaf pan. Allow dough to rise until double in size. Bake at 375 degrees for 25 minutes.

Vicky Eiben
Pleasant Fridge: Pleasant Ridge Waldorf School Community Cookbook

PARMESAN BUNDT ROLLS

$1/2$ package frozen unbaked yeast rolls (18)
$1/2$ cup (1 stick) butter, melted, divided
1 medium onion, finely chopped
1 teaspoon garlic powder
2 teaspoons dried parsley flakes
1 cup grated Parmesan cheese

Place frozen rolls on baking pan and brush lightly with 1 tablespoon of the melted butter. Cover loosely with plastic wrap and place in refrigerator overnight. Add onion, garlic powder, and parsley flakes to remaining 7 tablespoons butter. Roll dough in butter mixture then in cheese. Place in well-greased 12-cup Bundt pan. Cover loosely and let rise in a warm place until dough reaches the top of the pan. Bake in a preheated, 350-degree oven for 30 to 35 minutes. Turn out upside down on large platter and serve warm.

The Collection II: Simple & Elegant Recipes, Attic Angel Association

POTATO ROLLS

1 $1/2$ cups hot water
1 cup mashed potatoes
1 tablespoon salt
$3/4$ cup sugar
$2/3$ cup shortening, melted
2 eggs, beaten
2 packages dry yeast, soaked in $1/4$ cup warm water
About 7 $1/2$ cups flour

Stir the hot water into mashed potatoes; add salt, sugar, and melted shortening. When cool, add beaten eggs and yeast. Add flour gradually to form a soft but not sticky dough. Let rise until double. Knead dough and let rise again. Form into buns or rolls. Bake at 350 degrees for 25 minutes.

Linda (Kovars) Fischer
Castle Rock Lutheran Church Cookbook

If desired, salt may be cut in half.

GOOD PIZZA CRUST

2 teaspoons yeast
1 $2/3$ cups warm water
1 tablespoon honey or maple syrup
4 cups white flour
2 teaspoons salt
1 tablespoon dried rosemary

Combine yeast, water, and honey or maple syrup; let mix foam. Mix in flour, salt, and rosemary; then knead until you have a nice smooth ball. Let rise in a warm spot about an hour. Punch down and form 2 equal balls from the dough. Roll out on floured surface. Put on desired toppings. Bake the pizza at 425 degrees for 15 minutes or until done. Makes two 10-inch crusts.

Nancy Sky
Pleasant Fridge: Pleasant Ridge Waldorf School Community Cookbook

---

MOTHER'S BREAD PUDDING

  2 $1/4$ cups milk
  2 eggs, slightly beaten
  2 cups 1-inch bread cubes
  $1/2$ cup brown sugar
  $1/4$ teaspoon salt
  1 teaspoon vanilla
  1 tablespoon cinnamon
  $1/2$ cup raisins (optional)

Combine the milk and beaten eggs. Pour over the bread cubes and blend together. Blend remaining ingredients with bread-cube mixture. Pour into a buttered 8-by-8-inch baking dish and set dish in a shallow pan filled an inch deep with hot water, or pour into a buttered, covered casserole dish. Bake at 350 degrees about 35 to 40 minutes or until knife inserted into pudding comes out clean.

Marge Swalheim
A Table in the Wilderness, Western Koshkonong Lutheran Church

Recipe works well with 3 cups of bread cubes.

FRENCH TOAST STUFFED WITH BANANAS AND WALNUTS

  6 eggs
  $1/4$ cup half and half
  1 teaspoon vanilla
  $1/4$ teaspoon cinnamon
  4 ripe bananas, peeled and mashed
  $1/4$ cup coarsely chopped walnuts
  $1/8$ teaspoon nutmeg
  8 slices egg bread
  2 to 4 tablespoons butter
  Powdered sugar and walnut halves (optional)

In a medium bowl, beat eggs and stir in half and half, vanilla, and cinnamon. In a separate bowl, combine mashed bananas, chopped walnuts, and nutmeg. Spread banana mixture generously onto four slices of egg bread and cover each with remaining four slices of bread. In a medium saucepan, melt butter over medium heat. Dip sandwiches into egg mixture, turning until saturated on both sides. Place sandwiches into hot butter in saucepan and fry for about 2 minutes on each side. If desired, sprinkle with powdered sugar and garnish with walnut halves. Makes 4 servings.

Barb Van Der Hulst
Cooksville Lutheran Church Cookbook

BAKED APPLE FRENCH TOAST

 1 to 2 loaves French bread, about 1 pound
 8 eggs
 3 cups milk
 $^3/_4$ cup sugar, divided
 1 tablespoon vanilla
 5 Granny Smith apples
 2 teaspoons cinnamon
 2 tablespoons butter

Preheat oven to 400 degrees. Spray a 9-by-13-inch pan with vegetable oil spray. Slice bread into 1 $^1/_2$-inch thick pieces. Place bread tightly together in one layer at the bottom of the prepared pan. Place eggs in bowl and beat lightly. Add milk, $^1/_4$ cup of the sugar, and vanilla; mix with whisk. Pour half of the liquid over the bread. Peel, core, and cut apples into rings. Cover bread with apple rings, overlapping rings slightly. Pour remaining egg mixture over apples. Mix remaining $^1/_2$ cup sugar with cinnamon; sprinkle evenly over apples and dot with butter. Bake for 35 minutes. Cool for 5 to 10 minutes before serving with maple syrup. Makes 12 servings.

Carla Lynch
From Our House to Your House: Recipes from the Madison Curling Club

If toast is assembled in advance, cover and refrigerate overnight; increase baking time to 50 minutes. Recipe can be halved and baked in an 8-inch-square pan for 20 to 35 minutes.

DID YOU KNOW? GOOD COOKING TIPS FROM COMMUNITY COOKBOOKS

- To get more juice from a lemon, heat it in the microwave for about 10 seconds before extracting the juice.
- Cut-up pantyhose can sometimes be used in place of cheesecloth— just make sure they are clean!
- Rub a little butter over cheese, if you won't be using it right away, and it won't harden.
- Overly crispy cookies may have too much sugar or liquid in the dough.
- To prevent splashing when frying meat, sprinkle a little salt into the pan before putting in the fat.
- Add $1/4$ teaspoon baking soda to cranberries while cooking and they won't need as much sugar.
- To cut down on odors from cooking cabbage, cauliflower, etc., add a little lemon or vinegar to the cooking water.
- Ice cubes will help sharpen garbage disposal blades.
- Fresh tomatoes will keep longer if stored in the refrigerator with the stems down.
- A bit of celery in your bread bag will keep the bread fresher for a longer time.
- When using honey as a substitute for sugar, reduce the amount of liquids by $1/4$ cup per cup of honey in the conventional recipe.
- If you really like frosting (and extra layers), try cutting each layer in half lengthwise before applying frosting. Drag dental floss lengthwise through the layers; it's easier than using a knife.
- For juicer hamburger, add $1/2$ cup cold water to 1 pound of beef before grilling.

HEIDI'S TURNER HALL KASEKÜCHEN (CHEESE PIE)

6 eggs
2 cups cream
1 teaspoon salt
$^1/_4$ cup grated onion
3 cups grated Swiss cheese (not too sharp)
1 (9-inch) unbaked deep-dish pie shell

Preheat oven to 400 degrees. Beat eggs with cream, salt, and onion; fold in cheese and pour into pie shell. Bake at 400 degrees for 10 minutes, then at 350 degrees for 35 minutes. Serve hot, garnished with fresh fruit.

Gisela Halbheer
Old World Swiss Family Recipes, Monroe Swiss Singers

This is a unique and popular entree available in Monroe, Wisconsin, at Turner Hall, the home and headquarters of the Monroe Swiss Singers. I used a regular-sized pie shell when baking this and had enough to fill two of them.

SKILLET FRITTATA

3 tablespoons olive oil
2 $^1/_2$ cups chopped vegetables, including broccoli, red pepper, onion
    and mushrooms
2 cups frozen hash brown potatoes, defrosted
6 eggs
$^1/_4$ cup water
2 teaspoons Dijon mustard
1 teaspoon salt
$^1/_2$ teaspoon freshly ground black pepper
1 $^1/_4$ cups shredded cheddar cheese

Preheat broiler. Wrap handle of 10-inch nonstick skillet with foil. Place oil in pan and add vegetables and potatoes. Cook over medium heat for 5 minutes. Mix eggs, water, mustard, salt, and pepper, and pour over mixture in skillet. Cook until eggs are almost set. Sprinkle with cheese. Broil until cheese is melted. Serve immediately. Makes 4 to 6 servings.

A frittata is the Italian version of an omelet. They are usually cooked in a heavy skillet over low heat until firm, left open-face, not folded, and then placed in the oven or under the broiler to cook the top side.

The Collection II: Simple & Elegant Recipes, Attic Angel Association

CHEESE AND SPINACH STRATA

1 package (10 ounces) shredded sharp cheddar cheese, divided
2 packages (10 ounces each) frozen chopped spinach, thawed and squeezed dry
$^2/_3$ cup chopped onion
$^1/_2$ cup butter, softened
18 thinly sliced, firm white bread slices
4 eggs
4 cups milk
1 tablespoon prepared mustard
2 teaspoons salt
$^1/_4$ teaspoon pepper

Combine 2 cups of the cheese with the spinach and onion. Spread butter lightly on both sides of bread slices. Place about six slices of bread in the bottom of a 9-by-13-inch greased baking dish. Layer half the cheese mixture, about six bread slices, and the other half of the cheese-spinach-onion mixture on top. Cut remaining six bread slices into triangles and arrange over casserole. Sprinkle with remaining cheese. Beat eggs, milk, mustard, salt, and pepper; pour over casserole. Chill, covered, for 1 hour or longer. Overnight is best. Bake at 350 degrees for 60 minutes or until knife inserted in center comes out clean. Let stand for 15 minutes before cutting into squares. Makes 8 to 10 servings.

Variation: Substitute lightly cooked asparagus for the spinach.

Monica L. Hansen
From Our House to Your House: Recipes from the Madison Curling Club

GERMAN POTATO PANCAKES

2 cups grated raw potatoes, drained
1 egg, beaten
1 ½ tablespoons flour
½ teaspoon salt
2 tablespoons shortening

Grate potatoes and let stand in strainer to drain excess liquid (squeeze to drain more). Place grated potatoes into a bowl. Add beaten egg, flour, and salt. Drop by spoonfuls on hot griddle using just enough shortening to keep them from burning. Fry until brown on both sides. Serve hot with applesauce and sausages. Makes 2 to 4 servings.

Being of German heritage, these have been a favorite of my family and still are. I've eaten potato pancakes in many other places; this is the correct way to make them. You do not use much flour. On the first Sunday in May and October, there is a potato pancake breakfast in a tiny village, Tilleda, Wisconsin, in Shawano County. Hundreds come to this breakfast. The pancakes are the best!

Bea Moede
The Wisconsin Gardener Cookbook 3

DESSERTS

PUMPKIN AND CHOCOLATE CHIP COOKIES

1 can (15 or 16 ounces) pumpkin
2 cups sugar
1 cup vegetable oil
2 eggs
4 cups flour
4 teaspoons baking powder
2 teaspoons cinnamon
1 teaspoon salt
2 teaspoons baking soda, dissolved in 2 teaspoons milk
2 cups chocolate chips
1 cup chopped nuts
2 teaspoons vanilla

Combine pumpkin, sugar, oil, and eggs; beat well. Stir together flour, baking powder, cinnamon, and salt; add to pumpkin mixture along with dissolved baking soda and mix well. Stir in chocolate chips, nuts and vanilla. Drop by teaspoon on lightly greased cookie sheet. Bake at 375 for 10 to 12 minutes. Makes 10 dozen cookies.

Judy Robinson
The Catholic Communities of St. Andrew, Verona, and St. William, Paoli, Cookbook

WALNUT LEMON DROPS

For the cookies:

$1/_2$ cup butter
1 $1/_3$ cups sugar
1 cup plain or lemon yogurt
$1/_3$ cup lemon juice
2 $1/_4$ cups flour
1 teaspoon baking soda
1 teaspoon salt
$1/_2$ cup chopped walnuts

For the frosting:

1 package (3 ounces) cream cheese, at room temperature
2 tablespoons cream
$1/_2$ teaspoon vanilla
1 tablespoon soft butter
1 $1/_2$ cups powdered sugar

For the cookies, in a large bowl, cream butter and sugar. Blend in yogurt and lemon juice. Combine dry ingredients and add to butter mixture. Mix well. Stir in nuts. Drop by rounded teaspoonfuls onto a greased baking sheet. Bake at 350 degrees for 15 minutes. To make frosting, mix cream cheese, cream, vanilla, and butter together. Add powdered sugar and mix well. Frost cooled cookies.

Joan Hammond
Castle Rock Lutheran Church Cookbook

For firmer dough, use a 6-ounce container of yogurt rather than the 1 cup called for in the original recipe.

LIME COOLERS

2 $\frac{1}{2}$ cups all-purpose flour, divided
$\frac{1}{2}$ cup powdered sugar
$\frac{3}{4}$ cup cold butter
4 eggs
2 cups sugar
$\frac{1}{3}$ cup lime juice
$\frac{1}{2}$ teaspoon lime peel
$\frac{1}{2}$ teaspoon baking powder
Additional powdered sugar for topping

In a bowl, combine 2 cups flour and powdered sugar; cut in butter until mixture resembles coarse crumbs. Pat into a greased 9-by-13-inch baking pan. Bake at 350 degrees for 20 minutes or until lightly browned. In a bowl, whisk the eggs, sugar, lime juice and peel until frothy. Combine the baking powder and remaining flour; whisk in egg mixture. Pour over hot crust. Bake for 20 to 25 minutes or until light golden brown.

Cool on wire rack. Dust with powdered sugar. Makes 3 dozen bars.

Kerry Stoppleworth
Sharing Our Recipes: A Collection by the Park Elementary School PTA, Cross Plains

ORANGE PECAN COOKIES

1 cup butter (do not use margarine or shortening)
1 egg
$\frac{1}{2}$ cup brown sugar
$\frac{1}{2}$ cup sugar
1 tablespoon orange juice

1 tablespoon orange rind

$^1/_2$ cup pecans, dusted with flour

2 $^3/_4$ cups flour

$^1/_4$ teaspoon baking soda

Cream butter, egg, and sugars. Add orange juice and rind; add pecans. Beat well. Add flour with baking soda. Shape into rolls and wrap in waxed paper; chill well. Slice and bake at 350 degrees about 10 minutes until done (cookies do not brown on top). Makes 5 dozen cookies.

Evelyn Beyer
Cooksville Lutheran Church Cookbook

SALTED PEANUT COOKIES

1 cup butter

2 cups brown sugar

2 eggs, beaten

1 teaspoon baking soda

1 teaspoon baking powder

$^1/_2$ teaspoon salt

2 cups flour

2 cups quick-cooking oats

1 cup corn flakes

1 cup salted peanuts

Preheat oven to 350 degrees. Melt butter; add brown sugar. Add eggs; then add sifted dry ingredients. Fold in oats, corn flakes, and nuts. Drop from teaspoon onto greased cookie sheet. Bake 15 minutes. Cookies should still be a bit soft. Makes 4 dozen.

Judy Vasby
Family and Friends Cuisine, 2006. A Collection of Favorite Recipes from the Family and Friends of Willerup United Methodist Church

LEMON OAT LACIES

2 cups butter or margarine, softened

1 cup sugar

2 cups all-purpose flour

3 cups quick-cooking or old-fashioned oats, uncooked

1 tablespoon grated lemon peel
1 teaspoon vanilla
Powdered sugar

Beat butter and sugar until creamy. Add remaining ingredients except powdered sugar; mix well. Cover; chill 30 minutes. Heat oven to 350 degrees. Shape dough into 1-inch balls; place on ungreased cookie sheet. Flatten with bottom of glass dipped in powdered sugar. Bake 12 to 15 minutes until edges are light golden brown. Cool 1 minute on cookie sheet; remove to wire rack. Cool completely. Sprinkle with powdered sugar, if desired. Makes about 4 $^1/_2$ dozen cookies.

In memory of Irene Dauck
For Everything There is a Season, Vermont Lutheran Church, 150 Years of Faith, Fellowship and Food

---

RUSSIAN PASTRY SQUARES
$^1/_4$ pound (1 stick) margarine or butter
$^1/_2$ cup sugar
2 eggs, separated
1 teaspoon vanilla
1 $^1/_2$ cups flour
$^1/_8$ teaspoon baking powder
Pinch of baking soda
1 jar (10 to 12 ounces) raspberry preserves or orange marmalade
Chopped nuts

Preheat oven to 350 degrees. Cream margarine or butter and sugar; add egg yolks and beat until light and fluffy. Add vanilla, then dry ingredients (mixture will be crumbly). Pat into greased 9-by-13-inch pan. Spread with preserves and sprinkle with some of the chopped nuts. Beat the egg whites until they form soft peaks. Spread the egg whites; then sprinkle with remaining nuts. Bake for 25 minutes. Cut into 12 to 15 squares when cool.

Terry Gray
United Presbyterian Church 150th Anniversary Cookbook

SHARING OUR LOVE OF COOKING

Nancy Johnson, Terry Gray, and Laura Dougherty
United Presbyterian Church 150th Anniversary Cookbook

COOKING TIP

▶ To prevent garlic cloves from drying out, peel and place in a small jar. Cover with oil (olive is best) and store in the fridge. The oil picks up the garlic's scent and can be used when garlic infused oil is desired elsewhere.

▶ Sprinkle flour on bacon before frying to keep it from curling.

▶ A spoonful of powdered sugar added to whipped cream will enable it to be stored in the refrigerator without breaking down.

▶ Add flavor and thickening to stews with a little oatmeal or grated potato.

▶ A leaf of lettuce dropped into a pot will absorb grease off the top of a soup; remove lettuce and throw it away.

▶ After putting cake batter in a pan, lift the pan and drop it sharply to the table to release air bubbles. This will prevent the cake from falling (no kidding).

Nancy: I was raised on a farm in southern Michigan and I started cooking around age 12. My mother's family was French and my father's ancestors came from Germany. We were raised on meat, potatoes, and vegetables, and that is how we raised our kids as well. My grandmother was a great cook but she never wrote anything down. When asked about how to make her dishes, she always talked about adding a pinch of this and a pinch of that. Some of her outstanding dishes were an oyster soufflé and a great gingerbread cake, which we have tried to duplicate many times but it's just not the same.

Laura: I came from Stevens Point originally and was a home-economics graduate in the 30s. I'm 98 now and I still remember the wonderful pastries and fruit pies my Swiss mother made. I had two sisters and every day my mother would make a big, beautiful meal just for us.

Terry: My parents were born in Czechoslovakia, but my brother and sister and I were orphaned when I was still young. They were older and worked during the day, so I learned how to cook for them. I made many simple, one-pot meals with an eastern European flavor, such as cabbage rolls with sauerkraut and potato dumplings. I used to go to my Slavic girlfriend's house on Sundays and holidays. They had lots and lots of people over and fed all of them. Back then, the big heavy meal was at noon. We ate outside on their big front porch; it was usually a chicken or pork dinner. I still cook and like making pierogis for the holidays with prune, cottage cheese, or a sautéed fried-cabbage filling. I've had a few baking mishaps over the years. Once I mistook olive oil for lemon extract when I was making brownies. They were not too popular—in fact, no one would touch them.

MEXICAN WEDDING CAKES

    1 cup butter or margarine
    $1/_2$ cup powdered sugar
    1 teaspoon vanilla
    2 $1/_4$ cups flour
    $3/_4$ cup finely chopped nuts

Mix butter, sugar, vanilla, and flour thoroughly. Work nuts into dough until it holds together. Shape into walnut-sized balls. Bake on ungreased baking sheet 10 to 12 minutes at 400 degrees. While warm, roll into powdered sugar. Cool.

Peggy Korth
Family and Friends Cuisine, 2006. A Collection of Favorite Recipes from the Family and Friends of Willerup United Methodist Church

After cooling, cookies can be rolled in powdered sugar again.

JENNY DERER'S APRICOT PINWHEEL COOKIES

Cookie:
>1 cup butter
>1 cup sugar
>1 cup brown sugar
>3 eggs, beaten
>1 teaspoon vanilla
>5 cups flour
>$^1/_2$ teaspoon salt
>1 teaspoon baking soda

Filling:
>1 pound dried apricots, chopped
>$^1/_2$ cup sugar
>$^1/_2$ cup water
>1 cup nutmeats

For the cookies, cream butter and sugars; add beaten eggs, vanilla, flour, salt, and soda. Divide dough into 4 sections, rolling each section to $^1/_2$-inch thick.

For the filling, combine ingredients in saucepan and cook until thick. Cool. Spread on dough. Roll up like a jellyroll. Wrap in plastic wrap and store in refrigerator overnight.

Cut slices and bake on greased cookie sheet for 5 minutes at 425 degrees.

Bonnie Dauck
For Everything There is a Season, Vermont Lutheran Church, 150 Years of Faith, Fellowship and Food

---

SOUR CREAM CHOCOLATE COOKIES

>$^1/_2$ cup butter or margarine, softened
>$^3/_4$ cup sugar
>$^1/_2$ cup packed brown sugar
>1 egg
>$^1/_2$ cup sour cream
>1 teaspoon vanilla extract
>1 $^3/_4$ cups flour
>$^1/_2$ cup baking cocoa
>1 teaspoon baking soda
>$^1/_4$ teaspoon salt
>1 cup semisweet chocolate chips

114

Cream butter or margarine and sugars; add egg, sour cream, and vanilla. Gradually add dry ingredients. Stir in chips. Drop by tablespoonfuls onto greased baking sheet. Bake in 350-degree oven until set. Do not overbake.

Wilma Peterson
Castle Rock Lutheran Church Cookbook

GRANDMA FELLAND'S MOLASSES CRISP COOKIES

1 $^1/_2$ cups butter
2 cups sugar
$^1/_2$ cup dark molasses
2 eggs
4 teaspoons baking soda
4 cups flour
1 teaspoon cloves
1 teaspoon ginger
2 teaspoons cinnamon
1 teaspoon salt

Melt butter; cool. Add sugar, molasses, and eggs. Sift dry ingredients together and add to first mixture. Chill dough. Drop teaspoonfuls onto greased cookie sheets. Flatten with a glass that has been dipped in sugar. Bake at 375 degrees for 8 to 10 minutes.

Karen Harvey
A Table in the Wilderness, Western Koshkonong Lutheran Church

TEAMWORK

At least two generations of Fellands have been using this cookie recipe. It's a mom-and-pop operation, turning out 10-12 dozen of these much-loved cookies at a time for their family. They store the finished cookies in tins.

Dad rolled the small $^3/_4$-inch balls to be placed on the cookie sheet, and then Mom took over to thinly press the cookie ball with the bottom of a glass dipped in sugar. A generation ago, Gladys and Wynter Felland modeled this routine for daughter, Jan Harvey, who followed in her parents' pattern with her husband, Paul. Now Jan's daughter, Karen, is doing the same thing.

115

AWESOME COOKIES

1 cup butter

$^3/_4$ cup sugar

$^3/_4$ cup brown sugar

2 eggs

1 teaspoon vanilla

2 cups flour

2 $^1/_2$ cups oats, blended to a fine powder

$^3/_4$ teaspoon salt

1 teaspoon baking powder

1 teaspoon baking soda

12 ounces chocolate chips

8 ounces chocolate bar, grated (optional)

1 $^1/_2$ cups chopped nuts (optional)

Cream butter and both sugars. Add eggs and vanilla. Mix together with flour, oats, salt, baking powder and soda. Add chocolate chips, grated chocolate bar, and nuts. Roll into balls and place on a cookie sheet. Bake for about 10 minutes at 375 degrees. Makes 20 to 30 cookies.

Tom and Jean Westerhoff

Pleasant Fridge: Pleasant Ridge Waldorf School Community Cookbook

These cookies taste even better the next day. Substitute raw sunflower seeds for the nuts, if desired.

AWESOME BLOWOUTS

$^1/_2$ cup butter, softened

$^1/_2$ cup peanut butter

$^1/_2$ cup packed brown sugar

$^1/_4$ cup sugar

1 teaspoon baking soda

$^1/_4$ teaspoon salt

1 egg

$^1/_4$ cup milk

1 teaspoon vanilla

2 cups all-purpose flour

$^3/_4$ cup chocolate chips

$^3/_4$ cup honey-roasted peanuts

$^3/_4$ cup coarsely chopped, bite-size, chocolate-covered peanut-butter cups
(about 15)

In a large bowl, beat butter and peanut butter with mixer for 30 seconds. Add sugars, baking soda, and salt. Beat until well combined, scraping often. Beat in egg, milk, and vanilla. Using the mixer, beat in as much of the flour as you can. Stir in remaining flour by hand. Stir in chocolate chips, peanuts, and peanut-butter cups. Drop by generously rounded teaspoons, 2 inches apart on ungreased cookie sheet. Bake in a 350-degree oven for about 10 minutes or until lightly browned. Transfer to a wire rack to cool. Makes about 30 cookies.

For easier chopping, freeze peanut-butter cups in wrappers for 1 hour. Remove wrappings and chop.

Janet Krahn
United Presbyterian Church 150th Anniversary Cookbook

Substitute regular peanuts for honey-roasted peanuts or eliminate if recipe is too sweet. Kids love them.

AUNT CAROL'S LEMON-ZUCCHINI COOKIES

    2 cups flour
    1 teaspoon baking powder
    $1/_2$ teaspoon salt
    $3/_4$ cup butter
    $3/_4$ cup sugar
    1 egg, beaten
    1 teaspoon grated lemon peel
    1 cup zucchini, unpeeled and shredded
    1 cup walnuts, chopped
    1 cup powdered sugar
    1 $1/_2$ tablespoons lemon juice

Stir together flour, baking powder, and salt. Set aside. In a large mixing bowl, cream together butter and sugar. Add beaten egg and lemon peel; blend until fluffy. Stir in flour mixture until dough is smooth. Stir in zucchini and walnuts. Drop by rounded teaspoon onto a greased cookie sheet. Bake at 375 degrees for 15 to 20 minutes or until cookies are lightly browned. Place baked cookies on a cooling rack.

Mix together powdered sugar and lemon juice. Drizzle frosting over cookies while the cookies are still warm.

Jill Stone-Brisky

For Everything There is a Season, Vermont Lutheran Church, 150 Years of Faith, Fellowship and Food

These cookies are also delicious (and lighter) without nuts.

PEANUT BUTTER COOKIES

$1/2$ cup shortening

$3/4$ cup creamy peanut butter

1 $1/4$ cups packed brown sugar

3 tablespoons milk

1 tablespoon vanilla

1 egg

1 $3/4$ cups flour

$3/4$ teaspoon salt

$3/4$ teaspoon baking soda

Combine shortening, peanut butter, brown sugar, milk, and vanilla. Beat until well blended. Add egg and beat. Combine flour, salt, and baking soda; mix well. Add flour mixture to creamed mixture slowly. Mix until well blended. Drop teaspoonfuls onto ungreased baking sheets. Flatten with fork. Bake in preheated, 375-degree oven for 7 to 8 minutes or until just beginning to brown. Do not overbake. Cool 2 minutes on sheet before moving to cooling rack.

Dough can be shaped into balls before baking for a more evenly shaped cookie.

Michelle Gehrke

Castle Rock Lutheran Church Cookbook

COW PIES

1 $1/4$ cups butter

2 cups sugar

2 eggs

2 teaspoons vanilla

2 cups flour

$3/4$ cups cocoa

1 teaspoon baking soda

$1/2$ teaspoon salt

1 package (12 ounces) peanut-butter chips

Mix butter and sugar until light and fluffy; add eggs and vanilla. Beat well. Stir in flour, cocoa, baking soda, and salt. Stir in chips. Bake at 350 degrees on a greased cookie sheet for 9 to 11 minutes.

Rhonda Wethal
Cooksville Lutheran Church Cookbook

RASPBERRY SHORTBREAD COOKIES
Cookie:

> 1 cup butter, softened
> $^2/_3$ cup sugar
> $^1/_2$ teaspoon almond extract
> 2 cups flour
> $^1/_2$ cup seedless raspberry jam

Glaze:

> 1 cup powdered sugar
> $^1/_2$ teaspoon almond extract
> 2 to 3 teaspoons water

In a mixing bowl cream butter and sugar; beat in extract. Gradually add flour until dough forms a ball. Cover and refrigerate 1 hour or more. Roll into $^3/_4$-inch balls. Place 1 inch apart on ungreased baking sheets. Make a small well in the center of each cookie. Place raspberry jam in the well. Bake at 350 degrees for 12 to 15 minutes or until edges are lightly browned. Place pan on wire rack to cool.

Combine glaze ingredients; drizzle over cooled cookies. Makes about 3 $^1/_2$ dozen cookies.

Klover Schafer
For Everything There is a Season, Vermont Lutheran Church, 150 Years of Faith, Fellowship and Food

The quality of the jam or preserves is important in this recipe; one with reduced sugar tastes better. You can experiment with other flavors as well.

SUGAR COOKIES

> 3 cups flour
> $1/2$ teaspoon baking soda
> $1/2$ teaspoon baking powder
> Pinch of salt
> 1 cup (2 sticks) butter or margarine, softened
> 1 cup sugar
> 2 eggs
> 1 teaspoon vanilla
> Colored sugar

In a large bowl, combine flour, baking soda, baking powder, salt, and butter. Mix together until mealy. In smaller second bowl, mix 1 cup sugar, eggs, and vanilla. Mix thoroughly. Then add contents of small bowl to mixture in large bowl and mix well. Cover and refrigerate at least 2 hours or overnight. Roll to about $1/4$-inch thickness. Cut cookie shapes and shake on sugar. Bake at 350 degrees for 6 to 9 minutes.

Pearl Swiggum
Sharing Our Recipes: A Collection by the Park Elementary School PTA, Cross Plains

---

HIP PADDLERS

Crumb mixture:

> 1 cup sugar
> 1 egg
> $1/2$ teaspoon baking soda
> $1/2$ cup butter
> 1 $1/4$ cups flour
> 1 $1/2$ cups quick-cooking oatmeal

Filling:

> 1 teaspoon vanilla
> 1 can sweetened condensed milk (such as Eagle Brand)
> 2 tablespoons butter
> 1 cup chocolate chips

Combine crumb mixture ingredients. Place half of mixture in a 9-by-13-inch pan; reserve remaining mixture for top.

Combine filling ingredients in saucepan and heat to melt. Place filling on crumbs in pan. Top with remaining crumbs. Bake at 350 degrees for 15 minutes—no longer.

Karen Barnstable
Cooksville Lutheran Church Cookbook

PEARL SWIGGUM REMEMBERS

Pearl Swiggum, former columnist for the *Wisconsin State Journal,* is now 93 and lives in Gays Mills with her daughter, Marjie, and her scientific son-in-law.

When I was three years old, an influenza epidemic took our mother Golda, who was called Goldie. Our father, Sigurd Stevenson, had a country store in Towerville, and with my stepmother's permission, I walked every day about a mile to be with my Aunt Olla (called Ollie) Rogers. At her kitchen table was always a heavy glass sugar bowl and spoon holder. And near the table in the cupboard: a sugar-cookie jar. I was always allowed to help myself, even though her family rule was no snacking between meals. I walked with her up the valley alongside the cornfield to dig potatoes or pick peas. Then in the late afternoon, I walked the mile back to Towerville with cookies in my pockets to nibble on the way. Across the valley lived a big husky boy, one of a large family and the oldest. Tilman James Swiggum was his name, and when Uncle Elmer needed help, he became the hired man. I was in awe of him and never really got acquainted.

Some years later, my sister and I went to a Saturday night dance—every store out in the country held dances every Saturday night. I wasn't yet interested in boys. We girls always danced together, in fact even married women danced together; few men danced.

Then I began to notice this big bashful guy, who turned out to be Tilman, playing the accordion, never a smile on his face. I started to smile at him every time I danced past. One intermission, Tilman brushed past me on the way to the snack table and said in a real low voice, "Wanta go to the show Saturday night?" Of course, I said yes.

Getting married then was just going to the preacher with a couple to "stand up" for you. They were my sister and her boyfriend. Tilman and I eventually bought the Stump Ridge farm from my uncle. The house was a shack, but the barn came first so we upgraded that and then came the house. My son now owns the farm and my grandson who lives there lets me mow the yard all summer. My daughter drives me up there—it only takes two hours to mow. As soon as they came on the market, I bought a large-size Dixon mower—no shift. It's a piece of cake. I can hardly wait till summer.

ANNA'S GINGERBREAD

Gingerbread:

> 2 cups flour
> 1 cup sugar
> 2 teaspoons baking soda
> 1 teaspoon cinnamon
> 1 teaspoon cloves
> 1 teaspoon ground ginger
> 3 eggs
> 1 cup oil
> 1 cup molasses
> 1 cup hot water

Topping:

> Juice and zest of 1 orange
> $1/2$ to $3/4$ cup sugar, or to taste

For the gingerbread, sift dry ingredients. Put in bowl. Add the eggs, oil, and molasses and mix well. Add hot water last. Mix. Bake in a 9-by-13-inch pan 30 minutes.

For the topping, blend ingredients together. Poke holes in warm gingerbread with toothpick and spread orange-sugar mixture on top.

Katy Hougan
A Table in the Wilderness, Western Koshkonong Lutheran Church

Koshkonong Prairie veteran farmers Anna and Henry Hougan spent many retirement winters at their trailer home in Florida. During this time, Anna was inspired by the abundance of oranges and enhanced her gingerbread with an orange glaze topped by a dollop of whipped cream.

RHUBARB PIE BARS

Crust:

1 $^1/_4$ cups flour

6 tablespoons butter

$^1/_2$ cup powdered sugar

Filling:

3 cups rhubarb

3 eggs

$^3/_4$ cup sugar

$^1/_4$ teaspoon salt

$^1/_4$ cup flour

Preheat oven to 350 degrees. Combine flour, butter, and powdered sugar for the crust. Press into 9-by-13-inch pan and bake for 15 minutes. Remove from oven and let cool. Mix rhubarb, eggs, sugar, salt, and flour and spread on crust. Bake for 35 minutes.

Sheila Kupersmith
Pleasant Fridge: Pleasant Ridge Waldorf School Community Cookbook

---

CHOCOLATE MOUSSE TORTE

1 bar unsweetened baking chocolate

1 can sweetened condensed milk (such as Eagle Brand)

2 teaspoons vanilla

1 pint whipping cream

9-inch pie shell, baked

Combine chocolate, sweetened condensed milk, and vanilla; microwave on high for 2 to 4 minutes. Mix after every minute until melted and smooth. Cool to room temperature, about 1 $^1/_2$ hours. Beat cooled mixture to make sure it is smooth. Beat whipping cream until stiff and fold in chocolate mixture. Place in baked pie shell. Refrigerate until ready to serve.

Corky Shumway
United Presbyterian Church 150th Anniversary Cookbook

BANANA CHIP BARS

$^3/_4$ cup butter or margarine, softened

$^1/_2$ cup sugar

$^1/_2$ cup packed brown sugar

1 egg

1 teaspoon vanilla

2 ripe bananas, mashed (1 cup)

2 cups all-purpose flour, or 1 cup whole wheat flour plus $^3/_4$ cup all-
purpose flour and $^1/_4$ cup wheat germ

2 teaspoons baking powder

$^1/_2$ teaspoon salt

1 package (12 ounces) chocolate chips

Grease and flour a 10-by-15-inch jellyroll pan. Preheat oven to 350 degrees. Cream butter or margarine and sugars until fluffy. Add egg and vanilla; beat well. Stir in bananas. Stir together flour (or flours plus wheat germ), baking powder, and salt. Add to creamed mixture. Beat well. Stir in chocolate chips. Spread in prepared pan. Bake at 350 degrees for 25 minutes. Cool. Cut into 36 bars.

Pat Foltz
Cooksville Lutheran Church Cookbook

STRAWBERRY RHUBARB CRISP

2 cups sliced strawberries

4 cups diced rhubarb

1 cup granulated sugar, divided

2 teaspoons orange zest

2 tablespoons cornstarch

$^1/_4$ cup orange juice

9 tablespoons butter, cut into $^1/_2$ inch pieces

1 $^1/_4$ cups flour

$^1/_4$ cup brown sugar

$^1/_4$ teaspoon salt

Ice cream

Preheat oven to 375 degrees. Lightly grease a 10-inch, fluted quiche dish or pie pan. Combine strawberries, rhubarb, $^3/_4$ cup of the granulated sugar, orange zest, cornstarch, and orange juice. Mix thoroughly and place in prepared dish. Combine butter, remaining $^1/_4$ cup sugar, flour, brown sugar, and salt, until mixture is crumbly. Sprinkle this mixture evenly over fruit mixture. Bake for 45 minutes or until fruit is bubbly and crumb topping is brown around edges. Cool slightly and serve warm with ice cream.

The Collection II: Simple & Elegant Recipes, Attic Angel Association

Although this cookbook is full of rhubarb recipes, this one, a late addition, was so outstanding (some would call it magnificent) it had to be included.

FRESH PEACH PIE
  3 skinned, pitted fresh ripe peaches, mashed
  1 cup sugar
  4 tablespoons cornstarch
  $1/2$ cup cold water
  7 skinned, pitted fresh ripe peaches
  1 baked pie shell
  Whipping cream

Mix sugar and cornstarch, add water and the 3 mashed peaches and cook until thickened. Set aside to cool. Slice 7 skinned peaches and add them to the baked pie shell. Pour the sugar/cornstarch/peach mixture on top and put in refrigerator. Chill. Serve with real whipping cream on top.

Jodi Strasburg
Family and Friends Cuisine, 2006. A Collection of Favorite Recipes from the Family and Friends of Willerup United Methodist Church

SHINY TOP COBBLER
Cobbler:
  5 cups fruit (any kind)
  1 $1/2$ tablespoons lemon juice
  2 cups flour
  $1/3$ cup margarine
  2 teaspoons baking powder
  1 $1/2$ cups sugar
  $1/2$ teaspoon salt
  1 cup milk

Topping:
> 1 $^1/_2$ cups sugar
> $^1/_2$ teaspoon salt
> 2 tablespoons cornstarch
> 1 $^1/_2$ cups boiling water

Mix fruit and lemon juice in a 9-by-13-inch baking dish. Using a mixer and a separate bowl, mix flour, margarine, baking powder, sugar, salt, and milk together to make a smooth batter. Pour batter over fruit, spreading a little.

For the topping, in a smaller bowl, mix sugar, salt, and cornstarch. This is dry. Shake and pour over the batter on top of the fruit; pour boiling water over all in baking dish. Bake in preheated, 350-degree oven for 50 minutes to 1 hour or until crust is light brown. Toothpick should not come out doughy. Serve warm or cold.

Berries are great! I've tried strawberries, black caps, and blackberries. Peeled apples and peaches work nice, too!

Michelle Gehrke
Castle Rock Lutheran Church Cookbook

CRANBERRY BAKED DESSERT

Cake:
> 1 cup sugar
> 3 tablespoons butter, melted
> $^1/_2$ teaspoon salt
> 1 $^1/_4$ cups milk
> 2 cups flour
> 2 teaspoons baking powder
> 2 cups cut-up cranberries

Sauce:
> 8 tablespoons butter
> $^1/_2$ cup light cream
> 1 $^1/_2$ cups brown sugar

Mix all cake ingredients together, except cranberries. Gently stir in cranberries. Pour into 8-inch-square pan. Bake at 350 degrees for 45 minutes.

Heat sauce ingredients in double boiler until dissolved. Serve cake with hot sauce poured over it.

Trudy Stace
Cooksville Lutheran Church Cookbook

FILLED CHOCOLATE CUPCAKES

Cream-cheese mixture:

    1 package (8 ounces) cream cheese

    1 egg

    $1/_8$ teaspoon salt

    $1/_3$ cup sugar

    1 cup mini chocolate chips

Cupcake batter:

    1 $1/_2$ cups flour

    1 cup sugar

    $1/_4$ cup cocoa

    1 teaspoon baking soda

    $1/_2$ teaspoon salt

    1 cup water

    $1/_3$ cup oil

    1 tablespoon vinegar

    1 teaspoon vanilla

For the cream-cheese filling, combine cream cheese, egg, salt, sugar, and chocolate chips and set aside.

For the cupcake batter, combine flour, sugar, cocoa, baking soda, and salt. In a separate bowl, combine water, oil, vinegar, and vanilla. Add wet ingredients to dry ingredients. Mix well. Fill muffin cups half-full with batter. Top each with a heaping teaspoon of cream-cheese mixture. Bake at 350 degrees for 30 to 35 minutes. Do not be alarmed when they fall. Makes 2 dozen cupcakes.

Deb Rosen
United Presbyterian Church 150th Anniversary Cookbook

RHUBARB TORTE

Crust:

    1 cup flour

    2 tablespoons sugar

    Pinch of salt

    $1/_2$ cup butter

Filling:
>   1 ¹/₂ cups sugar
>   2 tablespoons flour
>   2 ¹/₄ cups rhubarb, cut fine
>   ¹/₃ cup cream
>   Rind of 1 orange, grated
>   3 egg yolks, beaten

Meringue:
>   3 egg whites
>   6 tablespoons sugar

For the crust, blend flour, sugar, salt, and butter. Place in bottom of 8-inch-square pan and bake at 350 degrees for 30 minutes or until brown.

For the filling, combine the sugar, flour, rhubarb, cream, orange rind, and beaten egg yolks; pour over baked crust. Bake at 350 degrees for 40 minutes.

For the meringue, beat egg whites and sugar until frothy. Spread over baked torte and bake an additional 15 minutes at 325 degrees.

Sue Brown
United Presbyterian Church 150th Anniversary Cookbook

Reduce sugar for a fuller, tarter flavor.

AL'S MOM'S GOOD CAKE
>   4 eggs, separated
>   4 tablespoons water
>   1 cup sugar
>   1 cup flour
>   1 tablespoon baking powder
>   1 teaspoon vanilla
>   Lemon filling or custard of your choice

Beat egg yolks with water until light. Add sugar, flour, baking powder, and vanilla. Beat egg whites and fold in. Bake in two greased, 9-inch round layer pans at 350 degrees for 25 minutes. Cool and split each layer. Fill with your favorite custard or lemon filling.

Ginny Johnson (in memory of Ruby Johnson)
For Everything There is a Season, Vermont Lutheran Church, 150 Years of Faith, Fellowship and Food

SOME THOUGHTS ON COOKING

Ginny Johnson
For Everything There is a Season, Vermont Lutheran Church, 150 Years of
Faith, Fellowship and Food

COOKING TIP

▶ My mother-in-law always picked out good fruit and used her
"sniffer" a lot. She used to smell bags of apples; the apples with a
good scent would taste good. I follow her example.

I grew up in a large family on a Wisconsin farm. We had a big garden, which fed my
family. There were five girls and we all learned to cook by listening to my mother,
Selma Lee. As she worked in the garden, she would holler directions at us through
the window. One of my jobs was to feed the chickens. The chicken feed was different then than it is now. We fed them ground-up oyster shells; it made the chicken's
eggshells strong, and they stayed fresh a long time. When you think of it, eggs come
in a nearly perfect package.

I liked to bake, and my husband, Al, was my guinea pig. He was always good-
natured about it, though. Al's mother, Ruby Johnson, was a good cook. She had
seven children and, even after they were grown, they liked to come home on
Sunday. She never knew who would show up, but somehow always knew how to
make a three-pound roast stretch to feed 14 people. She would go down to the basement and bring up a homemade can of this and a can of that and before you knew
it the table would be full. I don't know how she did it; it was almost like a miracle.

SLOW COOKER HOT FUDGE CAKE

1 3/4 cups packed brown sugar, divided
1 cup flour
1/2 cup unsweetened cocoa, divided
2 teaspoons baking powder
1/2 teaspoon salt
1/2 cup milk
2 tablespoons butter, melted
1/2 teaspoon vanilla
1 3/4 cups boiling water
Vanilla ice cream

Mix 1 cup brown sugar, flour, 3 tablespoons cocoa, baking powder, and salt. Stir in milk, melted butter, and vanilla. Spread over bottom of slow cooker. Mix together remaining brown sugar and remaining cocoa; sprinkle over mixture in cooker. Pour in boiling water. DO NOT STIR. Cover and cook on high 2 to 3 hours or until toothpick inserted comes out clean. Serve hot with vanilla ice cream.

Cindy Page
For Everything There is a Season, Vermont Lutheran Church, 150 Years of Faith, Fellowship and Food

This recipe is easy to assemble with impressive results—very handy for busy cooks with a little pre-planning.

BLACK FOREST CAKE

Cake:

> 4 ounces unsweetened chocolate
> 2 cups sugar, divided
> 1 $^1/_2$ cups buttermilk, divided
> 2 cups flour
> 1 $^1/_2$ teaspoons baking powder
> 1 teaspoon baking soda
> 1 teaspoon salt
> $^3/_4$ cup butter
> 3 eggs
> 1 teaspoon vanilla

Filling:

> 2 cans (20 ounces each) tart, pitted cherries, undrained
> 1 cup sugar
> $^1/_4$ cup cornstarch
> 1 $^1/_2$ teaspoons vanilla
> 3 cups cold whipping cream
> $^1/_3$ cup powdered sugar

For the cake, melt chocolate in saucepan over very low heat, stirring constantly until smooth. Add $^1/_2$ cup sugar and $^1/_2$ cup buttermilk. Stir until well blended. Cool thoroughly. Mix flour, baking powder, baking soda, and salt in a separate bowl and set aside. Cream butter; gradually beat in remaining 1 $^1/_2$ cups sugar and continue beating until light and fluffy. Add eggs, one at a time, beating thoroughly after each. Blend in about a fourth of the flour mixture. Blend in chocolate mixture and vanilla. Alternate adding remaining flour mixture and remaining 1 cup buttermilk, beating after each addition until smooth.

Pour into two greased and floured 9-inch cake pans. Bake at 350 degrees for about 35 to 40 minutes or until a cake tester inserted in center comes out clean. Cool in pans 10 minutes. Remove from pans. Finish cooling on racks.

For the filling, drain cherries, reserving $1/2$ cup juice. Combine reserved cherry juice, cherries, sugar, and cornstarch in saucepan. Cook and stir over low heat until thickened; add vanilla and stir.

To assemble, split each cake layer in half horizontally; crumble $1/2$ layer and set aside, leaving three layers for the cake assembly. Beat cold whipping cream and powdered sugar in a large bowl with an electric mixer. Set at a high speed until stiff peaks form. Reserve 1 $1/2$ cups whipped cream for decorative piping. Place one cake layer on serving plate. Spread with 1 cup whipped cream and top with $3/4$ cup cherry topping. Top with second cake layer, 1 cup whipped cream, and $1/4$ cup cherry topping. Top with third cake layer.

Frost the cake sides with remaining whipped cream and pat gently with reserved cake crumbs. Spoon reserved, 1 $1/2$ cup whipped cream into pastry bag fitted with star tip. Pipe around top and bottom edges of cake. Spoon remaining cherry topping over top of cake.

To get stiff peaks quickly with whipping cream, chill the mixing bowl and the beaters before beating cream. Also make sure the whipping cream is well chilled.

Margarethe Bayer, Kurt R. Kline
Old World Swiss Family Recipes, Monroe Swiss Singers

This is labor intensive but well worth it—a perfect special occasion cake.

HOME BAKED CHEESECAKE
Crumb crust:
    1 $1/2$ cups graham cracker crumbs
    $1/2$ cup butter

Filling:
    3 packages (8 ounces each) cream cheese, softened
    $3/4$ cup sugar
    $1/2$ cup sour cream
    2 teaspoons vanilla
    3 tablespoons all-purpose flour
    3 eggs
    Strawberries, for garnish

Preheat oven to 450 degrees. Prepare crust by placing graham cracker crumbs in a bowl. Melt butter and pour into bowl. Mix with crumbs; then pat mixture into bottom of springform pan.

For the filling, in a large bowl, beat together cream cheese, sugar, sour cream, and vanilla at medium speed until smooth. Gradually add flour, blending well. Add eggs, one at a time, beating well after each addition. Pour into springform pan and bake 10 minutes at 450 degrees. Reduce oven temperature to 250 degrees and continue baking for 30 minutes. Remove from oven. Cool to room temperature and refrigerate 2 hours or overnight. Remove side of springform pan. Garnish with strawberry slices and serve.

Linda (Kovars) Fischer
Castle Rock Lutheran Church Cookbook

An 8-inch-square or 9-inch-square pan can be substituted for the springform pan.

SWEDISH APPLE PIE

For the filling:
>   Sliced apples
>   2 tablespoons sugar
>   1 teaspoon cinnamon

For the topping:
>   1 cup flour
>   1 cup sugar
>   1 egg
>   1 stick butter, melted

For the filling, fill pie dish three-quarters full of sliced apples. Sprinkle with mixture of sugar and cinnamon.

Combine topping ingredients and put mixture on top of apples. Bake at 350 degrees for 45 minutes.

Esther Volkening
Recipes and Memories, Trinity Lutheran Church, Arkdale

THREE BERRY PIE

2 cups strawberries
2 cups raspberries
2 cups blueberries
1 cup plus 1 tablespoon sugar
$1/4$ cup cornstarch
$1/4$ teaspoon cinnamon
2 teaspoons lemon zest
1 teaspoon vanilla
Pastry for double-crust pie

Combine ingredients except crust and spoon berry mixture into chilled piecrust. Bake at 400 degrees for 1 to 1 $1/4$ hours.

Susan Schaub
For Everything There is a Season, Vermont Lutheran Church, 150 Years of Faith, Fellowship and Food

ZUCCHINI PIE

Unbaked 9-inch piecrust

Filling:

4 cups zucchini, peeled and sliced
1 $1/2$ teaspoons cream of tartar
Dash of salt
2 tablespoons flour
1 tablespoon lemon juice
Dash of nutmeg
1 $1/4$ cups sugar
$1^1/_2$ teaspoons cinnamon
1 teaspoon butter

Topping:

1 stick margarine or butter
$1/2$ cup sugar
1 cup flour

For the filling, cook zucchini for 10 minutes in small amount of water. Drain. Mix the rest of the filling ingredients together, except butter, and pour in unbaked piecrust; dot with butter.

133

Mix topping ingredients together using fork or pastry blender until crumbly. Sprinkle topping over pie. Bake at 375 degrees for 45 minutes.

Linda Hoffman

The Catholic Communities of St. Andrew, Verona, and St. William, Paoli Cookbook

This pie resembles apple pie.

RENA'S LEMON PIE

9-inch baked and cooked pie shell

Filling:

3 tablespoons cornstarch

2 cups water

1 scant cup sugar

Dash of salt

1 1/2 tablespoons butter

3 egg yolks, slightly beaten

1 large lemon

Topping:

3 egg whites

3 tablespoons sugar

Add cornstarch to water and the scant cup sugar. Bring to a boil. Add salt and butter and remove from heat. Add beaten egg yolks. Cool until thick. Add the juice of the lemon. Cool slightly before spooning into baked and cooled pie shell.

For the topping, beat egg whites until foamy, and slowly add sugar. Beat until stiff peaks form. Spread on top of pie and bake at 325 degrees until light brown.

Rena Fichter was our next-door neighbor. Our favorite treat was her wonderful lemon pie.

Jeanne Heideman

Recipes and Memories, Trinity Lutheran Church, Arkdale

GERMAN APPLE CAKE

Cake:

>2 large eggs or 3 small ones
>1 cup salad oil
>2 cups sugar
>1 teaspoon vanilla
>2 teaspoons cinnamon
>1 teaspoon baking soda
>$^1/_2$ teaspoon salt
>2 cups flour
>$^1/_2$ cup nuts
>4 cups thinly sliced apples

Cream-cheese frosting:

>2 small packages cream cheese
>3 tablespoons butter, softened
>1 $^1/_2$ cups powdered sugar
>1 teaspoon vanilla

For the cake, beat eggs and salad oil until light. Combine sugar, vanilla, cinnamon, soda, salt, and flour; add to egg-oil mixture. Then add nuts and thinly sliced apples. Bake in a 9-by-12-inch pan for 45 to 60 minutes at 350 degrees. Cool on wire rack.

Mix frosting ingredients until smooth. Spread on cooled caked.

Joanne Skalet (In memory of Mildred Skalet)
For Everything There is a Season, Vermont Lutheran Church, 150 Years of Faith, Fellowship and Food

CAKE IN THE TRUNK FROSTING

$^1/_4$ cup shortening

$^1/_4$ cup margarine

3 cups powdered sugar

2 tablespoons milk

$^1/_4$ teaspoon salt

$^1/_4$ teaspoon cream of tartar

1 teaspoon vanilla

1 egg white

Put ingredients in mixing bowl. Stir to moisten. Beat about 5 minutes with mixer. Add more powdered sugar, if needed.

Father Dave Timmerman likes this frosting. He wanted to bless my new car, so to show my gratitude, I baked him a cake frosted with this frosting. I put the cake in the trunk, and after he blessed the car I showed him the "special feature" in my trunk. He has since asked if I have a "cake in the trunk." And sometimes I do.

Carol Statz

The Catholic Communities of St. Andrew, Verona, and St. William, Paoli, Cookbook

PICNICS

Carol Statz

The Catholic Communities of St. Andrew, Verona, and St. William,
Paoli, Cookbook

I have three daughters and two daughters-in-law, who all have recipes in our church cookbook. My sons are fabulous cooks and bakers as well. We all love to bake and are skilled at making homemade breads and sweet rolls (yes, the yeast kind). Yeast does not intimidate us. We always have hot cross buns on Easter, made by my mother; she is 98 and still made them this year!

I grew up with family picnics. Both of my mother's parents had family reunions each year with picnic tables full of food. I went to a one-room country school, which had a card party one night a month. Certain people would be assigned to bring food. Two of my favorite foods were egg-salad and tuna-salad sandwiches (with the egg and tuna mixed together). Our family takes a trip to the Kickapoo Valley each year for apples—our "Apple Trip"—and has since 1971. The staple sandwich is the egg-tuna mix for some of us. At the end of the school year, we would have a family picnic. The food was always so good, but my absolute favorite was a rhubarb-meringue pie. I have tried numerous recipes, but I have never been able to find a recipe that tastes as good as that pie from my childhood.

Both my grandmothers were excellent cooks and bakers. My maternal grandmother always had huge jars of cookies sitting on a shelf along her basement stairs. When we went to Grandma's house, we could have cookies from those giant jars, whose covers were as big as our small hands. My paternal grandmother made cloverleaf rolls that were so light they could almost float in the air. And they would bake up so high—nearly four inches.

At our family gatherings now, everything is still homemade: truffles, pizza with homemade crusts, gourmet cinnamon rolls, homemade candies, cheesecakes. We enjoy making new recipes and sharing them with each other. For all of us, food is a creative outlet.

HERITAGE & ETHNIC SPECIALITIES

QUILT PATCHES

2 eggs
$^1/_2$ cup milk
2 teaspoons baking powder
$^1/_4$ teaspoon salt
2 cups flour
4 quarts chicken stock

Beat eggs and milk slightly with fork. Mix with all dry ingredients for a soft dough. Roll out on lightly floured board, 1/8-inch thick. Cut into 2-inch squares. Cook in boiling chicken stock for about 20 minutes. Makes 10 to 12 servings.

You can use any other stock, and also add meats and vegetables. My husband, Floyd, tells me that this is a recipe that he grew up with. My family of 13 had it once a month or more. It was a good staple meal. Floyd's mother, however, had to start her meal by going out to the chicken coop. It is a different form of chicken and noodle soup. You cut the noodles in squares or diamonds instead of noodle shapes. It is a little softer than noodle dough.

Bertilla LaMere
The Catholic Communities of St. Andrew, Verona, and St. William, Paoli, Cookbook

---

CHAMPINON SCHNITTEN (MUSHROOM TOAST)

1 pound mushrooms
$^1/_4$ cup onions, chopped
2 tablespoons butter
1 tablespoon flour
Salt and pepper
$^1/_4$ cup dry white wine
Some water
6 slices of bread

Cut mushrooms in small slices. Sauté onions and mushrooms with butter. Add flour, salt, and pepper. Slowly add wine; add water if needed and simmer for 10 to 15 minutes. Pour on toasted bread. Voila!

Daisy Peterson
Old World Swiss Family Recipes, Monroe Swiss Singers

BLITZ KUCHEN (LIGHTNING CAKE)

$1/_2$ cup butter or margarine

1 $1/_2$ cups sugar

3 eggs

4 tablespoons milk

1 $1/_2$ cup flour

1 $1/_2$ tablespoons baking powder

Topping (sprinkle on top):

Sugar

Nuts (almonds or walnuts)

Cinnamon

Cream butter or margarine and sugar; mix in eggs and milk. Sift in flour and baking powder, mix. Pour into greased and floured 9-by-13-inch pan. Add topping. Bake at 350 degrees for 30 minutes. Let cool and cut into bars.

Lois Pieper

A Table in the Wilderness, Western Koshkonong Lutheran Church

LIGHTNING CAKE

Before box cakes, panic would strike in the heart of a young bride who was warned of impending surprise company. If she were blessed with a recipe for a German stand by, *Blitz Kuchen* (lightning cake), the day would be saved. This recipe can be mixed and baked in short order. It has the advantages of being easy to make and also of being so delicious that you could eat half the cake at once.

This special mix of ingredients came into my life by way of my sainted mother-in-law, Bertha Pieper, who was a superb baker and cook. Her meals and baked goods were works of artistry. The German background in cooking and baking, learned in the kitchen of her mother, was the source of this woman's expertise. How many generations back these instructions had traveled to the present day, I do not know. Being a kitchen weakling, I am very happy to have been a recipient and have used this recipe often.

MOLSA

2 $1/_2$ gallons 2-percent milk

$1/_8$ teaspoon rennet (can be obtained from a cheese factory)

Bend a wire clothes hanger over the burner of a stove so it will hold a kettle above the burner. Use a big, heavy kettle. Place it on the hanger. Alice used her pressure cooker, which was cast-iron. Put 2 gallons of milk in this kettle and put it on very low heat so the milk is steaming. Start early in the morning, like 8 o'clock, and cook all day. Let it develop a light scum on top. Don't stir until late in the afternoon when testing for taste. Let it get lightly golden brown, but don't burn it. Put ¹/₂ gallon of milk in another kettle. Stir in the rennet and let it set. Curd will form and the whey will separate. Don't put in too much rennet or cheese will get tough. When cheese has formed, cut into chunks and add to first milk. Let all cook a little longer until all is golden brown. Chill before serving in bowls. May be kept for days in a cold place.

Alice Nelson
Castle Rock Lutheran Church Cookbook

Alice and Norman Nelson were very fond of molsa *and kept it on their north porch and ate it all winter. Norman brought Alice's* molsa *to a Castle Rock Brotherhood meeting when he was to serve the lunch, and all the men enjoyed it.*

MAKING THE COOKBOOK

Becky Nelson
Castle Rock Lutheran Church Cookbook

I grew up on a farm near Castle Rock. After college, I left and taught in military bases overseas in Europe and also in Japan, for quite a few years. This has given me quite a varied experience with cooking, and has made me open to trying new recipes.

I remember when I first started cooking, I wanted to surprise my mother and grandmother with a cake I made. The recipe called for a dash of salt. I wasn't sure what that meant, so I shook the salt in the shape and direction of a dash into the

batter. Of course, it came out much too salty. My mother laughed, but my grandmother ate it all up with a straight face, declaring it was the most wonderful cake she had ever had.

When we began putting together our cookbook for the sesquicentennial anniversary of our church, I wanted to collect recipes from some of our oldest members and from others who might have had recipes from deceased former parishioners. From these recipes and the stories behind them, you get a sense of what the day-to-day life in this community used to be. The recipe for *molsa*, a kind of milk soup with cheese curds in it, is an example of this. Another one is the recipe for *rommegrot* (butter mush). To get this one, and others, I brought cooking supplies and measuring tools and sat down with Clara Hoffland and her sister Sophia Svendsdo, and their lifelong friend Edna Hill, so we could re-create the recipes using more exact measurements. They were older women and could not see very well, so it was quite a challenge to get them to remember and visually re-create these dishes, but it was a lot of fun. This led me to seek out other members, sometimes in nursing homes, to contribute to the *Castle Rock Lutheran Church Cookbook*'s section of ethnic (and heritage) recipes. There are 7 recipes for *lefse* in the cookbook and many other old Norwegian, Scandinavian, and Welch recipes, as well as some from other lands.

Becky's passion and dedication for seeking out and saving these old recipes becomes apparent whenever you talk to her. She is one of the unsung heroes in preserving the dishes of the past.

LUTEFISK

2 ½ pounds air-dried fish, such as salt cod
1 cup slaked lime
2 quarts oak or maple ashes

Saw fish in 3 parts, clean thoroughly, and place in a wooden bowl or pail. Add water to cover and set in a cool place for 5 to 6 days. Change water several times. Remove fish and thoroughly clean wooden bowl. Make a solution of water, lime, and ashes and let it stand overnight. Drain off clear liquid and pour over soaked fish; set in a cool place for 7 days. When fish is soft, remove from solution, scrub bowl well, and soak fish for several days in clear cold water. Cook in salted water at simmering temperature for about 20 minutes. Drain well and serve. Allow ⅓ pound per person.

The Norwegians serve this fish with melted butter; the Swedes serve it with white or mustard sauce.

Evangeline Wearing
Castle Rock Lutheran Church Cookbook

DROMMER

1 cup butter
2 teaspoons vanilla
$^3/_4$ cup sugar
2 cups flour
1 teaspoon baking powder
36 whole blanched almonds (1 per cookie)

Cream butter and vanilla; add the sugar gradually, beating until fluffy. Blend flour and baking powder, adding dry ingredients to the butter-sugar mixture in four parts. If necessary, chill dough slightly, so you can roll into 1-inch balls. Place balls on cookie sheet and press almond into center of each cookie. Bake at 325 degrees for 20 to 25 minutes or until cookies are lightly browned and set.

Vermont Women ELCA
For Everything There is a Season, Vermont Lutheran Church, 150 Years of Faith, Fellowship and Food

KOLACHKY COOKIES

1 cup butter or margarine
1 package (8 ounces) cream cheese
3 tablespoons sugar
$^1/_4$ teaspoon salt
2 cups flour
Solo-brand filling works best: apricot, almond or your choice

Cream butter or margarine, cream cheese, sugar, and salt. Gradually add flour. Chill in refrigerator for an hour. Roll on floured pastry cloth until $^1/_8$ inch thick. Cut in 3-inch squares.

Put filling in center and bring corners together at center. Bake on greased cookie sheet at 350 degrees until golden brown.

Marge Waller
Recipes and Memories, Trinity Lutheran Church, Arkdale

Poppy seed and cherry also work well. This is one variation of a Kolachky pastry; another follows.

MOM'S CZECH KOLACHES

Dough:

    2 packages ($^1/_4$ ounce each) active dry yeast

    $^1/_2$ cup warm water (110 to 115 degrees)

    2 $^1/_2$ cups warm milk (110 to 115 degrees)

    $^3/_4$ cup sugar

    $^3/_4$ cup butter, softened

    2 teaspoons salt

    4 eggs

    11 cups all-purpose flour (can add an extra $^1/_2$ cup if needed), divided

Filling:

    2 cans (21 ounces) cherry pie filling or any type of Solo-brand filling

    $^1/_2$ cup sugar

    2 tablespoons cornstarch

    2 tablespoons cold water

Topping:

    1 package (8 ounces) cream cheese, softened

    $^2/_3$ cup sugar

    1 egg yolk

    Butter, melted

To make the dough, in a large mixing bowl dissolve yeast in warm water. Add milk, sugar, butter, salt, eggs, and 5 cups of flour; beat until smooth. Stir in enough remaining flour to make a very soft dough. Do not knead. Cover and let rise in a warm place until doubled, about 75 minutes. Meanwhile make filling.

For the filling, in a saucepan, combine pie filling and sugar. Combine cornstarch and cold water until smooth; stir into filling. Bring to a boil over medium heat. Cook and stir for 1 minute or until slightly thickened; set aside.

Turn dough onto a well-floured surface. Shape into 1 $^1/_2$ inch balls. Place 2 inches apart on greased baking sheets. Cover and let rise until doubled, about 40 minutes.

For the topping, in a mixing bowl, beat cream cheese, sugar, and egg yolk until smooth. Using the end of a wooden spoon handle, make an indentation in the center of each dough ball. Fill with 2 rounded teaspoons of filling. Make small indentation in center of filling; add 1 teaspoon of topping. Bake at 400 degrees for 10 to 15 minutes or until lightly browned. Brush melted butter over rolls. Remove from baking pans to wire racks to cool. Refrigerate leftovers. Makes about 6 dozen.

Darlene Hovorka (In memory of my mother, Mary Rezebek)
Recipes and Memories, Trinity Lutheran Church, Arkdale

An old time Czech tradition was to make kolaches *before the wedding and deliver them to the guests as an invitation. They were supposed to be an example of the great cooking skills of the future bride.*

LEFSE

Equipment needed:
> Lefse grill, capable of 500 degrees (keep clean)
> 30-inch long, ³/₄-inch diameter willow stick
> 24-inch long, ³/₄-inch flat, *lefse* turning stick
> Grooved *lefse* rolling pin with clean sock cover
> 30-by-30-inch clean rolling cloth of heavy cotton
> Potato ricer
> Cooling racks

Ingredients:
> 10 pounds Wisconsin Burbank Russet potatoes
> 12 tablespoons melted shortening, butter or margarine
> ²/₃ cups evaporated milk (1 small can)
> 4 teaspoons sugar
> 4 scant teaspoons salt
> 4 scant cups flour for initial batch
> 4 cups flour or as needed, for rolling

Procedure:
Peel and boil potatoes the same day *lefse* is made. Boil potatoes in salted water until firm, not soft. Drain potatoes and return pot to stove. Allow excess water to steam away for a minute or two, being careful not to burn potatoes. Remove potatoes from heat. Let stand for 2 minutes. Rice potatoes 2 times and measure out 12 cups. Combine potatoes, shortening, milk, sugar, and salt. Mix well. Place cupfuls of mixture on cookie sheets and cover with dry dishtowel. Place sheets on cooling racks. Cool at 40 to 50 degrees (not in refrigerator) for 2 hours. Note: This is a good time for a cup of coffee!

Put cooled potato mixture and 4 scant cups of flour in mixing bowl and mix with hands. Do not mix too much or gluten will form, making the batch sticky and ruining it. Form 2-inch diameter balls of dough, place on cookie sheets touching one another, cover with dry towel, and let stand for 20 minutes. Note: Have another cup of coffee!

Work a thin layer of flour into rolling pin sock and rolling cloth. Knead first ball of dough in hands, form into a thick pancake and start rolling process. Do not put pressure on the rolling pin; let the weight of the rolling pin do the work. Turn *lefse* several times during rolling process, by picking up edge of cloth and flipping *lefse* onto your arm. While holding *lefse* with one hand/arm you can flour the cloth with the other hand. Continue until *lefse* reaches proper thickness; diameter of *lefse* should be approximately the size of the grill. Wind up the *lefse* on the willow stick and unwind it on the grill. If the temperature is right, it should take about 1 minute for the *lefse* to cook. Turn the temperature down 25 degrees if the grill is too hot and *lefse* is developing dark brown spots too fast. Turn the *lefse* several times with the *lefse* stick during the cooking, checking constantly to see if the desired tenderness has been achieved. Excess flour should be dusted off *lefse* with a rag while it is cooking.

When *lefse* is done, use *lefse* stick to quarter-fold the *lefse* . Place 2 towels on cooling rack, place *lefse* on the towels, and cover with another 2 towels. As additional *lefse* is made, pile in layers, staggering the *lefse*, keeping square corners on the outside and overlapping the rounded edges 2 or 3 inches. Cover the stack of *lefse* with 2 towels. Do not place more than 18 *lefse* in a single stack. Keep the completed stacks of *lefse* tightly covered for 2 hours. Note: Yes, it is time for another cup of coffee and if you haven't already done what needs to be done: Do it now!

Spread several towels on table and place a single layer of the quarter-folded *lefse* on the towels. Allow *lefse* to cool for 5 to 10 minutes, until no longer warm to the touch. Do not allow *lefse* to sit too long or it will harden. Fold *lefse* once more and wrap 6 *lefse* in plastic wrap. Place in plastic bag and tie shut. Keep refrigerated for up to 4 days otherwise freeze until you want to use the *lefse* .

Last note: Try to plan it so you have at least 1 *lefse* per worker left over to consume fresh. Butter the *lefse*, shake a generous mixture of cinnamon and sugar over it, and enjoy with another cup of coffee.

Myrella Wilkins
For Everything There is a Season, Vermont Lutheran Church, 150 Years of Faith, Fellowship and Food

MEMORIES OF MYRELLA, THE "LEFSE QUEEN"

Ginny Johnson
For Everything There is a Season, Vermont Lutheran Church, 150 Years
of Faith, Fellowship and Food

Myrella Wilkins passed away last August; she was the *lefse* chairperson of our church for years and years and years. She was dubbed the "Lefse Queen." She and her husband, Otto, made and sold lefse for many years. Otto raised the potatoes, Myrella rolled the *lefse*, and Otto baked them.

KAPPELER MILK SOUP

> 2 ¹/₂ cups milk
> ¹/₂ teaspoon salt
> Nutmeg to taste
> 1 bay leaf
> 1 clove
> 4 egg yolks
> ¹/₃ cup cream
> Bread cubes, fried to a golden brown, in butter

Bring milk with seasonings to a boil; then cook on low heat, stirring constantly for a few minutes. Beat together the egg yolks and cream. Mix a little of the hot milk into the egg mixture, stirring constantly; then return to the milk, again stirring constantly until it is just about to boil. Season to taste. Add fried bread cubes, sprinkling over the top.

A proverb says, "If you land in the soup, you should also spoon it out." If two enemies both land in the soup and spoon it out together, a truce can come of it. Anyway, that's the story about the Milk Soup, which is said to have brought peace in the first Kappeler war of 1529 to the warring soldiers of the five Catholic areas of central Switzerland and the Zurich Reformed Movement.

Ida Leuenberger
Old World Swiss Family Recipes, Monroe Swiss Singers

BRÄTZELI

Deborah Krauss Smith, Director
Monroe Swiss Singers

Having a paternal grandmother from Switzerland and growing up in an area with a strong Swiss-immigrant influence, I never thought twice about the foods we ate. It wasn't until I was an adult and out in the world a bit that I realized how unique our foods were to our area. One thing, however, I knew was special, even as a child—making the Swiss cookie called *Brätzeli.* The simple dough, which is made basically of butter, sugar, flour, and eggs, is formed into small balls. The balls are then placed on a specially made iron and pressed to make an imprint on both sides of each cookie. The best-made *Brätzeli* are barely browned and very thin…perhaps only an 1/8 inch thick. Only four cookies can be made at a time, so it is a labor-intensive process and generally reserved only for Christmastime or other special occasions.

My mother, enlisting the help of my two siblings and me for *Brätzeli*-making, used my grandmother's iron, a heavy cast iron press from Switzerland that is placed over a burner. The upper and lower plates of the iron each have four pictures representing something about Switzerland. The pictures are imprinted on the

cookies when baked, so both sides of each cookie have a different picture of Switzerland on it. Some of the pictures I recognized and realized the significance of—like the alpine flower, Edelweiss—but some I didn't. As a kid, seeing those pictures on the iron made Grandma's homeland seem both a little unreal and a little magical. Years later as an adult, I traveled to Switzerland and actually visited some of the places I had seen (and eaten!) on those cookies, like the Weeping Lion stone monument in Lucerne *Brätzeli* and the twelfth-century Castle of Chillon. Although presently I own a new electric iron (which imprints only a design, not a picture) in addition to my grandmother's iron, I still almost exclusively use Grandma's old cast iron press for the making of *Brätzeli.* The new iron has no history or meaning to me, while the old iron connects me to fond memories of my dear Swiss grandmother, *Brätzeli*-making memories from my childhood, and my own Swiss heritage.

GROSSMUTTER'S BRÄTZELI

    1 cup butter
    1 $1/2$ cup sugar
    4 eggs
    1 teaspoon vanilla
    Pinch of salt
    Flour

Cream butter and sugar until fluffy. Add remaining ingredients, using enough flour to make a soft ball. Mix well. Too much flour will cause cookies to be tough and thick and too much egg may cause the cookies to lose detail in the iron. Roll dough into balls; place one ball on each section of the Brätzeli iron. Cook until lightly browned, approximately 5 minutes. Cookies made on old cast iron presses need to be turned to brown each side of the cookie.

This was the Brätzeli recipe of my grandmother, Emma Schär Krauss, who immigrated from the canton Aargau, Switzerland, in 1921 as a young woman.

Deborah Krauss Smith
Old World Swiss Family Recipes, Monroe Swiss Singers

NORWEGIAN PANCAKES

    3 eggs
    1 $1/2$ cups milk
    $1/2$ cup cream
    1 cup flour
    $1/4$ teaspoon salt
    2 tablespoons sugar
    $1/4$ cup butter or margarine, melted

Beat eggs until creamy. Add milk and cream; blend. Add dry ingredients. Beat and continue beating while adding melted butter or margarine. Pour $1/4$ cup batter on griddle and fry as regular pancakes. Serve folded or rolled with jam or jelly.

Marvel Martinsen
For Everything There is a Season, Vermont Lutheran Church, 150 Years of Faith, Fellowship and Food

OLD-TIME APPLE DUMPLINGS

2 cups sifted flour
2 teaspoons baking powder
$^1/_2$ teaspoon salt
$^1/_2$ cup shortening
$^2/_3$ cup milk
6 baking apples
$^1/_3$ cup sugar
$^1/_4$ teaspoon cinnamon
1 tablespoon butter
Milk

Sift together flour, baking powder, and salt; cut in shortening. Stir in milk; mix until a soft dough is formed. Place on flat surface and knead lightly. Roll $^1/_2$-inch thick and then cut into 6 squares. Peel, core, and slice apples, placing 1 apple on each square. Sprinkle each apple with sugar, cinnamon, and $^1/_2$ teaspoon butter. Moisten edges and press corners over apples. Brush with milk; place seam down. Bake at 350 degrees until tender.

Jeanette Woolever
Family and Friends Cuisine, 2006. A Collection of Favorite Recipes from the Family and Friends of Willerup United Methodist Church

GREAT-GRANDMA BURGER'S THICK STUFF

2 cups milk
$^1/_2$ cup flour
$^1/_4$ cup sugar
1 egg
$^1/_2$ teaspoon vanilla
Toast

Heat milk to almost boiling. Whisk in flour and sugar. In a separate bowl, beat egg. Whisk some hot mixture into egg, then whisk egg mixture back into hot mixture. Bring to a boil. Add vanilla and remove from heat. Cut toast into bite-size pieces and spoon mixture over them. Eat while watching cartoons on Saturday morning. Enjoy!

Brianna Kuchenbecker
The Catholic Communities of St. Andrew, Verona, and St William, Paoli, Cookbook

SWEDISH MEATBALLS

2 eggs, beaten
1 cup milk
$\frac{1}{2}$ cup dry breadcrumbs
3 tablespoons butter or margarine
$\frac{1}{2}$ cup chopped onion
1 pound ground chuck
$\frac{1}{4}$ pound ground pork
1 $\frac{3}{4}$ teaspoon salt
$\frac{3}{4}$ teaspoon dill weed
$\frac{1}{4}$ teaspoon allspice
$\frac{1}{8}$ teaspoon nutmeg
$\frac{1}{8}$ teaspoon cardamom
$\frac{1}{8}$ teaspoon pepper
3 tablespoons flour
1 can (10 $\frac{1}{2}$ ounces) beef broth
$\frac{1}{2}$ cup light cream

In a large bowl, combine the eggs, milk, and dry breadcrumbs. In a large skillet, heat 1 tablespoon butter or margarine; sauté chopped onion until soft. Lift out with a slotted spoon. Add to breadcrumb mixture, along with ground chuck and pork, 1 $\frac{1}{2}$ teaspoons salt, dill weed, allspice, nutmeg, and cardamom. With a wooden spoon or with your hands, mix well. Cover and refrigerate until very well chilled (this part is very important).

Shape meat mixture into small balls, about 1 inch in diameter. Preheat oven to 325 or 350 degrees. In remaining hot butter, sauté meatballs until browned. Remove meatballs to a 2-quart casserole as they are browned. Remove the skillet from the heat. Pour off drippings and add more butter, if necessary. Pour back into skillet; add flour, the remaining salt, and pepper, stirring together to make a smooth mixture. Gradually stir in beef broth; bring mixture to boiling, stirring constantly. Add cream. Pour over meatballs in casserole. Bake, covered, 30 minutes. Garnish top of meatballs with fresh sprigs of parsley, if desired.

Harriet Copus
Castle Rock Lutheran Church Cookbook

TURKISH LAMB STEW

4 Chinese eggplants or 1 medium American eggplant, peeled
$^1/_2$ cup olive oil
1 pound lamb, cut in 1-inch cubes (New Zealand lamb is best)
1 $^1/_2$ cups chopped onion
1 can whole tomatoes, quartered, plus juice
1 handful chopped parsley
4 fresh thyme sprigs
2 fresh marjoram sprigs
1 bay leaf
2 cans chicken stock
2 roasted green peppers, chopped in chunks

Cut eggplant into cubes, salt, and soak in cold water. Rinse and pat dry with paper towels. Add 3 tablespoons olive oil to stew pot and brown lamb pieces, about 20 minutes. Add onions and 2 more tablespoons of olive oil, sauté together until onions are golden, about 5 minutes. Stir in tomatoes, herbs, bay leaf, salt, pepper, and 1 $^1/_2$ cans of stock. Keep liquid level; adjust with extra stock. After about 30 minutes, add peppers. Brown eggplant in additional olive oil, and add to pot. Cook all for about 45 minutes more or to taste.

What makes this an especially tasty stew is that each ingredient gets sautéed or simmered a bit before other ingredients are added, so each flavor remains distinctive but is blended with others in the final step. Also the liberal use of good olive oil gives a richness like no other. Finally, the New Zealand lamb, which is grass fed, tastes just like the lamb my mom cooked when I was a kid. Insist on lamb, not mutton. My mom-in-law told me how much she enjoyed this stew, so I thought I would share it.

Susan Moss Hoffland
Castle Rock Lutheran Church Cookbook

The eggplant can be soaked for about an hour to get the bitterness out.

PASTY (CORNWALL, ENGLAND)

Crust:

>   2 cups flour
> $^2/_3$ cup shortening
>   4 tablespoons (or more) ice water
> $^1/_2$ teaspoon salt

Combine ingredients and chill.

Pasty:

>   2 $^1/_2$ cups peeled diced potatoes
>   2 cups peeled diced rutabagas
>   2 cups peeled diced carrots
>   1 large yellow onion
>   1 to 2 pounds ground meat
>   Salt and pepper to taste
>   Other seasonings you may like

Brown meat and onion on stovetop while you parboil potatoes, rutabaga and carrots. Season both to taste. Let cool. Combine both mixtures for filling.

Remove dough from the refrigerator and warm to room temperature. Roll out a baseball-size piece of dough into an oblong shape. Put about 1 $^1/_2$ cups of filling on half of the dough and close the pasty by pinching the edges, with the filling inside. Cover edges with aluminum foil and bake in a preheated 400 degree oven for 20 minutes, then remove foil and bake for another 25 minutes or until the crust is brown. Yield: 16 to 20 servings.

These can go right into the oven from the freezer, although it may take longer to cook.

Gillian (Folitz) Pakula
Castle Rock Lutheran Church Cookbook

Turnips can be used in place of rutabagas.

FRUKT SUPPE (FRUIT SOUP)

8 to 10 prunes
1 cup raisins
1 lemon, cut up
1 orange, cut up
$^1/_2$ cup sugar
3 tablespoons tapioca
Dash of cinnamon

Combine prunes, raisins, lemon, and orange in a saucepan. Cover with water and cook until softened. After mixture is cooked, add remaining ingredients and cook a little while longer. Serve warm or cold.

Many years ago, this "soup" was given to women who had just given birth, probably at home. The neighbor ladies would bring *frukt suppe* to the new mother and stay for a visit. As a child, when I was sick, my mother, Eleanor Hanson, would make it for me. I loved the taste, and it seemed to have great healing powers.

Cynthia McVay
Passed down from Eleanor Hanson, *Castle Rock Lutheran Church Cookbook*

TRES LECHES CAKE

8 large eggs
1 $^1/_2$ cups sugar
2 cups all-purpose flour
1 tablespoon baking powder
1 (14 ounce) can sweetened condensed milk
1 (12 ounce) can evaporated milk
1 cup milk
$^1/_4$ cup Kahlua liqueur (or strong coffee)
1 teaspoon vanilla
Whipped cream, lightly sweetened
Sliced strawberries

In a large bowl, with a mixer on high speed (use whip attachment if available), beat eggs and sugar until thick and pale yellow, 5 to 6 minutes.

In a small bowl, mix flour and baking powder. With mixer on medium speed, gradually add flour mixture in small increments and beat until smooth. Scrape batter into a buttered 9-by-13-inch baking pan. Bake at 325 degrees until a toothpick inserted into the center comes out clean, about 30 to 40 minutes.

Meanwhile, in a blender, whirl condensed milk, evaporated milk, regular milk, Kahlua or coffee, and vanilla until well blended. Pour evenly over hot cake; let cool for about 15 minutes, then cover and chill until cake has absorbed all the milk mixture, at least 3 hours or up to 1 day. Cut cake into squares, lift out with a wide spatula and set on plates. Top each piece of cake with a spoonful of whipped cream and garnish with strawberries.

Also called Three Milk Cake. The three milks when combined create just the right sweetness, density, and "mouth feel" for a rich cake, making it moist but not mushy. The cake is like one big giant sponge soaking up the delicious milk syrup. It is thought by most historians to have come from Nicaragua. This cake is very popular in Nicaragua, Mexico, Cuba, Puerto Rico, and Guatemala.

Mike LaMantia
Cooksville Lutheran Church Cookbook

PFEFFERNUSSE
    1 cup brown sugar
    1 cup shortening
    $^3/_4$ cup molasses
    $^3/_4$ cup honey
    2 to 3 large eggs ($^1/_2$ cup)
    1 $^1/_2$ teaspoons baking soda
    1 teaspoon salt
    $^1/_2$ teaspoon cinnamon
    $^1/_2$ teaspoon cloves
    $^1/_2$ teaspoon anise oil
    6 cups flour
    Powdered sugar

In a large sauce pan combine brown sugar, shortening, molasses, and honey and bring to a boil. Cool. Combine remaining ingredients, except for the powdered sugar, together and add to molasses mixture. Chill for at least 3 hours. Remove from refrigerator and roll dough into balls. Bake in a 375-degree oven for 10 to 12 minutes. Remove from oven and when still hot, roll each piece in powdered sugar. Store these cookies in a tightly covered container.

These cookies get even better with age.

Gertrude Soddy
Old World Swiss Family Recipes, Monroe Swiss Singers

EXTRA HELPINGS

ON WISCONSIN!

For a food-themed dinner reflecting some of the culinary delights of our state, choose from the following recipes. Dairy and cheese dishes are so ubiquitous that they are not listed here.

CRANBERRIES

Acorn Squash Stuffed with Apples and Cranberries, page 42

Apricot Cranberry Bread, page 87

Cranberry Baked Dessert, page 126

Cranberry Chutney, page 160

Cranberry Dip (Hot and Spicy), page 4

Cranberry Pound Cake, page 83

BRATS

Beer Brats, page 161

Brats with Sauerkraut Relish, page 160

Cheese 'N Brat Soup, page 21

WILD RICE

Almond Wild Rice, page 48

Creamy Wild Rice Soup, page 23

BEER

Beer Beef Stew With Dumplings, page 57

Beer Brats, page 161

Tomato Curry Chicken, page 62

ROSE PETAL JELLY

    2 cups water
    3 cups unsprayed pink rose petals (remove the thicker tissue at the base
      of the petals)
    2 $^1/_2$ cups sugar
    $^1/_4$ cup freshly squeezed lemon juice
    3 ounces of liquid pectin
    1 tablespoon rose water

Bring the water to a boil in a medium saucepan; remove from heat. Add petals; cover and steep for 30 minutes. Strain liquid into a clean saucepan; discard petals. Add sugar and lemon juice to pan. Bring mixture to a boil, stirring over medium high heat. Boil 2 minutes, then add pectin and boil another 2 minutes (for firmer jelly, boil up to 2 minutes more). Remove from heat; add rose water. Pour into sterilized jars and let cool completely. Store in refrigerator for up to 6 months. Yield 3 $^1/_4$ cups.

From Our House to Your House: Recipes from the Madison Curling Club

DANDELION WINE

    1 gallon of dandelion flowers (16 cups)
    1 gallon boiling water
    3 oranges

3 lemons

3 pounds sugar

1 ounce yeast

Pick dandelions early in the morning, taking care that no particles of the bitter stem are attached. Pour boiling water over the flowers. Let mixture stand 3 days. Strain. Cut the oranges and lemons into small pieces. Add the sugar, orange and lemon pieces, and yeast to dandelions. Let stand and ferment 3 weeks. Strain and bottle. Drink later.

Marion Nelson

Castle Rock Lutheran Church Cookbook

There are a lot of variations on this recipe, and though the basic ingredients are the same, they do involve alternative preparations for the oranges and lemons used. Some require peeling them with no pith remaining, some suggest using the rind, others require coarse grating of the peel of the oranges and lemons, and still others suggest thinly slicing them. Anyone adventurous enough to make dandelion wine will be inspired to experiment here.

KITCHEN SINK CHILI: CLEAR OUT THE FRIDGE/GARDEN/FREEZER

For the basic chili:

3 cups beans, any variety, cooked

1 quart tomatoes (fresh, frozen or canned), whizzed up in a blender or food processor until desired consistency

2 to 3 cups bulgur or TVP (texturized vegetable protein), or 1 to 2 pounds of ground venison, turkey or beef

1 to 2 tablespoons apple cider vinegar

3 tablespoons brown sugar or honey

Bragg's Liquid Aminos or salt to taste

Cumin

Chili powder

2 jalapeño peppers or any hot peppers, fresh or ground, to taste

Fresh cilantro

For the kitchen sink additions:

Various fresh or frozen vegetables

Olive oil (optional)

Put the basic chili ingredients together in a large pot or 6-quart Crock-Pot.

Here's where the "kitchen sink" part comes into play: Add 1 pint of frozen or 3 fresh sweet peppers, 1 pint frozen corn, and 1 pint frozen edible in-the-pod peas. Whiz them together in a food processor until desired consistency. Carrots, celery, or green beans are tasty as well. If desired, sauté vegetables in olive oil before adding. Bring everything to a boil; then turn down to a simmer for a couple of hours, stirring occasionally. If using a Crock-Pot, put it on high until it is bubbling, then turn it down to low. Taste things periodically and make adjustments, if necessary. Tasting is the best way to guarantee great results.

This recipe is as varied as what I have on hand. I am not a measurer unless I have to have exact measurements for baking.

Beth Walker Stephenson
Pleasant Fridge: Pleasant Ridge Waldorf School Community Cookbook

This recipe offers another good way to use up zucchini.

CRANBERRY CHUTNEY

1 (16-ounce) package cranberries
1 cup water
1 cup sugar
$1/_2$ cup orange juice
1 cup white raisins
1 cup walnuts
1 cup celery, diced
1 apple, chopped
$1/_2$ to 1 teaspoon ground ginger

Boil together the cranberries, water, and sugar for 15 minutes. Stir often. Add the orange juice, raisins, walnuts, celery, chopped apple, and the ginger. Cook for 10 minutes longer. Refrigerate.

Mary Sweeney
The Catholic Communities of St. Andrew, Verona, and St. William, Paoli, Cookbook

BRATS WITH SAUERKRAUT RELISH

$1/_4$ cup sugar
$1/_2$ teaspoon prepared mustard
$1/_4$ cup vinegar
$1/_8$ teaspoon garlic powder
$1/_8$ teaspoon pepper
1 8-ounce can sauerkraut, drained
$1/_4$ cup chopped green or red sweet pepper

$^1/_4$ cup cucumber, chopped
$^1/_4$ cup chopped onion
8 cooked bratwurst
Buns

Combine sugar and mustard in bowl. Stir in vinegar, garlic powder, and pepper. Stir in sauerkraut, sweet pepper, cucumber, and onion. Transfer to a container, cover and chill at least 2 hours or up to 2 days. Spoon about 1/4 cup relish on each brat. Serve with buns. Makes 8 servings.

Ruth Strassburg
From Our House to Your House: Recipes from the Madison Curling Club

BEER BRATS

8 bratwurst
1 can beer
1 large onion, sliced

Put 1 can of beer and 1 $^1/_2$ cans water and 1 sliced onion into a pot; simmer over low heat. Put in the brats to par-cook. When the brats are firm, cook them on outdoor grill until brown. Once brown, replace them into the beer mixture. When fully cooked, serve on a bun, top with onions.

Haxel Gelbach
Old World Swiss Family Recipes, Monroe Swiss Singers

DEVILS ON HORSEBACK

1 pound chicken livers
Butter
Salt and pepper
24 walnut or pecan halves
24 prunes, seeded
24 slices bacon

Sauté the chicken livers in butter, then cut into $^3/_4$-inch cubes. Salt and pepper to taste.

Stuff each prune with a slice of chicken liver and a walnut half. Wrap each prune with a bacon slice and secure with a wooden pick. Grill for 5 minutes or until bacon is crisp. Serve hot. Yield: 24 servings.

Mike LaMantia
Cooksville Lutheran Church Cookbook

BAKED PUMPKIN SEEDS

1 $^3/_4$ teaspoon Worcestershire sauce

2 tablespoons melted butter

2 cups pumpkin seeds

1 teaspoon salt

Leave pumpkin seeds unwashed with shells left on but fibers rubbed off. Combine ingredients in shallow pan. Stirring frequently, bake at 250 degrees for 2 to 3 hours, until dry. Cool, then store in tightly covered container.

Mike LaMantia

Cooksville Lutheran Church Cookbook

BARK CABIN GROUSE

2 grouse, cut into serving pieces

Flour, seasoned with salt and pepper

2 tablespoons butter

2 tablespoons cooking oil

1 $^1/_2$ cups white wine

$^1/_2$ cup orange juice

$^1/_2$ teaspoons rosemary leaves

$^1/_2$ teaspoon dry mustard

Pinch of ground red pepper

Douse bird pieces with seasoned flour. Brown in butter-oil mixture in a heavy skillet. Add wine, orange juice, rosemary, mustard, and red pepper to skillet. Cover and simmer for 1 $^1/_2$ hours. Add a little water, if necessary. Thicken sauce with a little flour and serve with hot buttered noodles. Serves 4.

Dena Levihn

From Our House to Your House: Recipes from the Madison Curling Club

VENISON SCALOPPINE DI BUE CON CAPPERI

8 thin slices of venison fillet

Salt and pepper

Nutmeg

Flour

5 tablespoons butter

1 tablespoon olive oil

$^1/_4$ cup capers

1 tablespoon chopped parsley

2-3 tablespoons wine vinegar

Pound meat until $^1/_2$ inch thick. Season with salt, pepper, and nutmeg. Coat with flour and brown in butter with oil. Add capers and parsley and 2 tablespoons cold water. Cook 5 minutes. In another pan, boil down wine vinegar to 1 tablespoon. Pour over meat, mix. Venison is best served rare to medium, as it is a very lean meat that toughens and develops a strong flavor if overcooked.

My wife was never a big venison fan. I tried dozens of recipes and this is the one she looks forward to most.

David Heath

Pleasant Fridge: Pleasant Ridge Waldorf School Community Cookbook

---

GRANDPA'S VENISON STEW

2 pounds venison, cut into small cubes

$^1/_4$ cup butter

$^1/_2$ cup flour

6 slices bacon, cut up

2 onions, diced

2 carrots, grated

2 stalks celery, chopped

1 can consommé (more if needed)

1 small jar red currant jelly

$^1/_2$ cup goat cheese, grated

1 cup sour cream

Salt and pepper

Brown slightly floured venison in butter, set aside. Cook bacon in a frying pan; remove bacon pieces. In remaining bacon grease, sauté onions, carrots, and celery on low for 30 minutes. Return bacon to pan. Add meat and rest of ingredients, except sour cream. Stir until sauce is blended and smooth. Cover and simmer 1 to 3 hours, or until meat is tender. Add sour cream, heat without boiling, and serve.

Bonnie Mansfield

From Our House to Your House: Recipes from the Madison Curling Club

SHEFADA (GREEK BEEF STEW)

>   3 pounds stew meat, cut in cubes (can use venison)
>   2 teaspoons salt
> $^1/_2$ teaspoon pepper
>   2 teaspoons oil
>   1 small can tomato paste
> $^1/_2$ cup red wine
>   1 teaspoon brown sugar
>   2 $^1/_2$ pounds onions, sliced
>   1 garlic clove
>   1 bay leaf
>   1 cinnamon stick
> $^1/_2$ teaspoon cloves

Put all ingredients in Crock-Pot and cook all day. Good for venison and tougher cuts of meat. Can be served with noodles, rice, or mashed potatoes.

Louise Thomas
Recipes and Memories, Trinity Lutheran Church, Arkdale

It is not specified in the recipe, but I would use the low setting for 8 to 10 hours.

HEAVENLY VENISON MEATBALLS

>   2 cups grated raw potatoes
>   1 $^1/_2$ pounds ground venison or ground beef
> $^2/_3$ cup chopped onion
>   1 $^1/_2$ teaspoon salt
> $^1/_8$ teaspoon pepper
> $^1/_4$ cup milk
>   1 egg
> $^1/_4$ cup butter
>   3 cups water
>   2 to 3 tablespoons flour
>   2 cups sour cream
>   1 teaspoon dill seeds
>   1 (10 ounce) package frozen peas, cooked

Combine potatoes, venison or ground beef, onion, salt, pepper, milk, and egg; shape into 1 $^1/_2$ inch balls. Brown in butter in large skillet. Add $^1/_2$ cup water; cover and simmer until done, about 20 minutes. Remove meatballs. Stir in flour, then remaining water. Simmer to thicken. Reduce heat, stir in sour cream and dill. Add meatballs and peas. Heat, but do not boil. Makes 8 servings

Judy Manteufel
A Table in the Wilderness, Western Koshkonong Lutheran Church

---

DOG BISCUITS

1 cup whole wheat flour
$1/2$ cup all-purpose flour
$3/4$ cup nonfat dry milk powder
$1/2$ cup wheat germ
$1/4$ cup cornmeal
$1/4$ cup honey
2 teaspoons garlic powder
1 egg, slightly beaten
1 cup beef or chicken broth

Mix flours, powdered milk, wheat germ, and cornmeal; add honey and garlic powder. Mix until crumbly. Add the beaten egg; gradually add canned broth, mixing until dough is like piecrust. May need to add some water or may not use all the broth. Roll dough out onto a well-floured board. Use cookie cutters or cut into desired shapes. Place in microwave for 5 to 10 minutes, until firm and dry. Rotate plate and turn treats over every 2 minutes. Watch carefully; microwaves vary in their heat settings. Cool on wire rack. Cookies crisp as they cool. May also roll dough into log shapes.

Shirley Butt
Cooksville Lutheran Church Cookbook

CONTRIBUTING COOKBOOKS

Castle Rock Lutheran Church Cookbook, Fennimore, Wisconsin

Compiled by: The parishioners of Castle Rock Lutheran Church in Fennimore to celebrate their church's 150th anniversary. Proceeds to benefit the church's WELCA program, which supports local and worldwide charities.

Contents: Features 242 pages of recipes with 8 categories, including a historical overview of Castle Rock and how food preparation and trends have changed in the community over time. Many of these recipes were keepsakes from previous generations and were contributed in the memory of family members and friends. A fascinating "Ethnic Section" features primarily Norwegian entrees.

Cost: $10 plus shipping. Contact Becky Nelson at 608-943-6924.

The Catholic Communities of St. Andrew, Verona, and St. William, Paoli, Wisconsin

Compiled by: St. Andrew's Council of Catholic Women with material submitted by parishioners, family, and friends of St. Andrew's and St. William's. Proceeds will be contributed to the St. Andrew's Endowment Fund.

Contents: Features more than 800 recipes on 370 pages in a 3-ring, vinyl binder that converts to an easel. Many standout dishes, including Viennese Plum Cake, Cauliflower-Walnut Casserole, Roquefort Lamb Chops, Charleston She Crab Soup, Custard Peach Pie, and Fresh Fruit Pandowdy.

Cost: $12 plus $4 shipping. Contact Carol Statz at 608-845-9333.

The Collection II: Simple & Elegant Recipes, Attic Angel Association, Madison, Wisconsin

Compiled by: Attic Angel Association members, with the proceeds going to support their mission. Attic Angels is a not-for-profit, independent organization of volunteers who improve the quality of life within Dane County. Their major focus is Attic Angel Community, which provides living and health care options for older adults.

Contents: An 8-by-11-inch, beautifully designed, soft cover bound book that was published in response to the overwhelming success of the first Attic Angel cookbook, *The Collection. The Collection II* features 249 pages of both easy-to-prepare comfort foods and recipes for entertaining with an international flavor. Chapters include Appetizers, Soups, Salads, Vegetables, Grains & Pasta, Entrees, Breads, and Desserts.

Cost: $19.95. The cookbook can be picked up from the Attic Angel Association at 640 Junction Road, Madison, WI 53717, or ordered from the office. For shipping costs and additional information, call the Attic Angel Association office at 608-662-8900 or visit their Web site, www.atticangel.org.

Cooksville Lutheran Church Cookbook, Evansville, Wisconsin

Compiled by: The Church Cookbook Committee, with material submitted by church members, family,

and friends. Proceeds to help make the historic church handicapped accessible.

Contents: This well-organized cookbook contains 375 spiral-bound pages, divided into eight sections with an index and a detailed church history. Includes a wide range of recipes, with multiple versions for popular dishes and a large dessert section.

Cost: $15 plus $3.50 shipping, with checks payable to Cooksville Lutheran Church. Send orders to Evelyn Beyer, 740 Brown School Road, #207, Evansville, WI 53536.

Family and Friends Cuisine, 2006. A Collection of Favorite Recipes from the Family and Friends of Willerup United Methodist Church, Cambridge, Wisconsin

Compiled by: The Women of Willerup United Methodist Church. Proceeds to be used for inner-city mission work throughout the United States.

Contents: More than 100 pages of recipes and around 20 pages of helpful tips from church members of the oldest Scandinavian Methodist church in the world (established in 1851). Features both a detailed church history and an extensive and helpful tip section.

Cost: $10 plus $4 shipping. For details on ordering, call Jeanette Retzlaff at 608-423-3360, or write to Jeanette at W9113 Red Feather Drive, Cambridge, WI 53523.

For Everything There is a Season, Vermont Lutheran Church, 150 Years of Faith, Fellowship and Food, Wisconsin

Compiled by: The Sesquicentennial Cookbook Committee, present and past church members, and friends. Proceeds will be used for local and international outreach projects, such as Equal Exchange and small farmer partners in Latin America, Africa, and Asia.

Contents: Handsomely spiral-bound, washable hardcover book, with 211 pages of recipes, which, in addition to the usual categories, includes a special section on Heritage Recipes and This and That. Some are from an era described as being "a time [that] regulated ovens were unknown, being fed by wood," and when "cake recipes were without the benefit of refined cake flour or other present day aids."

Cost: $15 plus $3 shipping. For purchase details, call Shirley Brandt 608-767-3030 or write her at 4670 Cedar Hill Lane, Black Earth, WI 53515.

From Our House to Your House: Recipes from The Madison Curling Club, Madison, Wisconsin

Compiled by: Members of the Madison Curling Club. Proceeds will help support Curling Club activities.

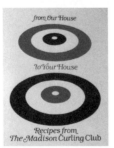

Contents: A 250-page, softcover, spiral-bound cookbook with more than 600 recipes in eight categories, which range from simple beverages to elaborate main dishes and desserts. The front pages contain a history of the Madison Curling Club.

Cost: $15 plus $4.50 shipping, or you can arrange to pick up a copy. To order send a check or money order (payable to Madison Curling Club) to Madison Curling Club, 4802 Marsh Road, McFarland, WI 53558, or call 608-444-6043.

Old World Swiss Family Recipes, Monroe Swiss Singers, Monroe, Wisconsin

Compiled by: Monroe Swiss Singers with proceeds to benefit the mission of preserving and perpetuating Swiss folk culture and music.

Contents: Second edition of authentic Swiss and German recipes from the home recipe files of the Monroe Swiss Singers, many of which have been used for generations. Examples of this are Dandelion Salad, Cheese Pie, Sauerbraten, Swiss Apple Omelet, Rhubarb Streusel, and Black Forest Cake.

Cost: $8.50 plus $2.50 shipping (please write or e-mail for postage rates for multiple copies) through *Old World Swiss Family Recipes*, c/o N4512 Cold Springs Road, Monroe, WI 53566, or e-mail info@MonroeSwissSingers.org.

Pleasant Fridge: Pleasant Ridge Waldorf School Community Cookbook, Wisconsin

Compiled by: The parents, staff, and friends of Pleasant Ridge Waldorf School in southwestern Wisconsin. Proceeds will be used for school-related activities, especially gardening and the hot lunch program.

Contents: A beautifully designed and illustrated 200-page, softcover, spiral-bound book from a school noted for being the first in Wisconsin to offer an organic hot lunch program. A short description of the Waldorf school history and philosophy opens the book, which contains six sections and recipes handed down over generations, as well as contemporary ones. Most of the recipes use fresh and natural ingredients.

Cost: $18 plus $2 shipping (if ordered in groups of 6 or more, cookbooks and postage are $18 each). To order, contact the school directly at 608-637-7828 or info@pleasantridgewaldorf.org.

Recipes and Memories, Trinity Lutheran Church, Arkdale, Wisconsin

Compiled by: The Trinity Lutheran Church Women's Cookbook Committee. Proceeds to benefit church youth functions and to help modernize the church's kitchen.

Contents: A 202-page, spiral-bound, softcover book featuring family keepsake recipes as well as contemporary items. Many of the dishes are dedicated to memories of the contributors' mothers and grandmothers.

Cost: $12 (includes shipping). Send payment and order to Trinity Lutheran Church, 1650 Church St., P.O. Box 65, Arkdale, WI 54613. For further information, call Susan O'Leary at 608-564-7920.

Sharing Our Recipes: A Collection by the Park Elementary School PTA, Cross Plains, Cross Plains, Wisconsin

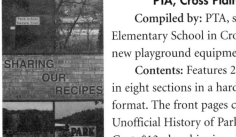

Compiled by: PTA, staff, and families of the Park Elementary School in Cross Plains. Proceeds will be used for new playground equipment.

Contents: Features 282 pages packed full of recipes in eight sections in a hardcover, washable, spiral-bound format. The front pages contain an interesting "Brief and Unofficial History of Park School [established in 1873]."

Cost: $12 plus shipping. Available at World of Variety in Cross Plains or by mail through Laurie Delmore at 798-4011 or LDelmore@chorus.net.

A Table in the Wilderness, Western Koshkonong Lutheran Church, Cottage Grove, Wisconsin

Compiled by: Luther Circle, a women's group from the Western Koshkonong Lutheran Church between Cottage Grove and Stoughton. Proceeds to support the Luther Circle projects for aiding church youth.

Contents: Features 116 pages with historic photos. This is a compilation of two former cookbooks (and many new items) in response to many requests for out-of-print recipes. A special section at the end is devoted to traditional church recipes or Koshkonong heritage cuisine.

Cost: $15 (includes shipping). Make checks out to Western Koshkonong Luther Circle at 2632 Church St., Cottage Grove, WI 53527.

United Presbyterian Church 150th Anniversary Cookbook, Wisconsin Dells, Wisconsin

Compiled by: The Women of the United Presbyterian Church, who note

"Nothing is better to cook than those recipes that have survived many years." Proceeds to be used for mission projects such as senior or shut-in meals and Port St. Vincent, a men's shelter.

Contents: Spiral-bound, washable book, with tabbed sections containing more than 100 recipes, some of which have been handed down for generations.

Cost: $10 plus $1 shipping. For details on ordering, call Nancy Johnson at 608-393-4952 or write to Nancy at 3946 9th Drive, Wisconsin Dells, WI 53965.

The Wisconsin Gardener Cookbook 3, Wisconsin Public Television

Compiled by: Cooks and gardeners from throughout Wisconsin, using

Wisconsin produce. Judges with a professional culinary background chose the recipes. To be considered for judging a recipe: must use Wisconsin produce for at least one of the ingredients, must appeal to the general public, and must have directions that are easy to follow, with preparation being under one hour. *The Wisconsin Gardener*, a series that airs four times a year on Wisconsin Public Television, was the inspiration for the cookbook. Proceeds will be used for Wisconsin Public Television funding.

Contents: A great bargain for a gorgeously produced, easy-to-read, softcover, wire-bound book of a little more than 75 pages, divided into six categories.

Cost: Only $5 plus $2 shipping for 1-2 cookbooks ($3 shipping for 3-4 cookbooks, and $4 shipping for 5 or more cookbooks). To order, visit the Wisconsin Public Television's Web site at wpt.org/garden and follow the prompts, or enclose a check made out to TV Extras by mail (along with your address, name, and daytime phone number, and number of cookbooks needed). Send this to *The Wisconsin Gardener Cookbook 3*, 821 University Ave., Madison, WI 53706-1412.

INDEX

MORE GREAT TITLES FROM TRAILS BOOKS

Activity Guides

Biking Illinois: 60 Great Road and Trail Rides, *David Johnsen*
Biking Iowa: 50 Great Road and Trail Rides, *Bob Morgan*
Biking Wisconsin: 50 Great Road and Trail Rides, *Steve Johnson*
Great Iowa Walks: 50 Strolls, Rambles, Hikes and Treks, *Lynn L. Walters*
Great Minnesota Walks: 49 Strolls, Rambles, Hikes, and Treks, *Wm. Chad McGrath*
Great Wisconsin Walks: 45 Strolls, Rambles, Hikes, and Treks, *Wm. Chad McGrath*
Paddling Illinois: 64 Great Trips by Canoe and Kayak, *Mike Svob*
Paddling Iowa: 96 Great Trips by Canoe and Kayak, *Nate Hoogeveen*
Paddling Northern Minnesota: 86 Great Trips by Canoe and Kayak, *Lynne Smith Diebel*
Paddling Northern Wisconsin: 82 Great Trips by Canoe and Kayak, *Mike Svob*
Paddling Southern Minnesota: 85 Great Trips by Canoe and Kayak, *Lynne and Robert Diebel*
Paddling Southern Wisconsin: 82 Great Trips by Canoe and Kayak, *Mike Svob*
Walking Tours of Wisconsin's Historic Towns, *Lucy Rhodes, Elizabeth McBride, Anita Matcha*
Wisconsin's Outdoor Treasures: A Guide to 150 Natural Destinations, *Tim Bewer*
Wisconsin Underground, *Doris Green*

Travel Guides

Classic Wisconsin Weekends, *Michael Bie*
Great Indiana Weekend Adventures, *Sally McKinney*
Great Iowa Weekend Adventures, *Mike Whye*
Great Midwest Country Escapes, *Nina Gadomski*
Great Minnesota Taverns, *David K. Wright & Monica G. Wright*
Great Weekend Adventures, *the Editors of* Wisconsin Trails
Great Wisconsin Taverns: 101 Distinctive Badger Bars, *Dennis Boyer*
Great Wisconsin Winter Weekends, *Candice Gaukel Andrews*
Minnesota Waterfalls, *Steve Johnson and Ken Belanger*
Tastes of Minnesota: A Food Lover's Tour, *Donna Tabbert Long*
The Great Indiana Touring Book: 20 Spectacular Auto Trips, *Thomas Huhti*
The Great Iowa Touring Book: 27 Spectacular Auto Trips, *Mike Whye*
The Great Minnesota Touring Book: 30 Spectacular Auto Trips, *Thomas Huhti*
The Great Wisconsin Touring Book: 30 Spectacular Auto Tours, *Gary Knowles*
Twin Cities Restaurant Guide, *Carla Waldemar*
Wisconsin Family Weekends: 20 Fun Trips for You and the Kids, *Susan Lampert Smith*
Wisconsin Lighthouses: A Photographic and Historical Guide, *Ken and Barb Wardius*
Wisconsin Waterfalls, *Patrick Lisi*
Up North Wisconsin: A Region for All Seasons, *Sharyn Alden*

Home and Garden

Creating a Perennial Garden in the Midwest, *Joan Severa*
Design Your Natural Midwest Garden, *Patricia Hill*
Eating Well in Wisconsin, *Jerry Minnich*
Midwest Cottage Gardening, *Frances Manos*
Northwoods Cottage Cookbook, *Jerry Minnich*
Wisconsin Almanac, *Jerry Minnich*

Wisconsin Country Gourmet, *Marge Snyder & Suzanne Breckenridge*
Wisconsin Garden Guide, *Jerry Minnich*
Wisconsin Wildfoods: 100 Recipes for Badger State Bounties, *John Motoviloff*

Sports

After They Were Packers, *Jerry Poling*
Always a Badger: The Pat Richter Story, *Vince Sweeney*
Baseball in Beertown: America's Pastime in Milwaukee, *Todd Mishler*
Badger Sports Trivia Teasers, *Jerry Minnich*
Before They Were the Packers: Green Bay's Town
Team Days, *Denis J. Gullickson and Carl Hanson*
Boston Red Sox Trivia Teasers, *Richard Pennington*
Chicago Bears Trivia Teasers, *Steve Johnson*
Cold Wars: 40+ Years of Packer- Viking Rivalry, *Todd Mishler*
Detroit Red Wings Trivia Teasers, *Richard Pennington*
Green Bay Packers Titletown Trivia Teasers, *Don Davenport*
Mudbaths and Bloodbaths: The Inside Story of the Bears-
Packers Rivalry, *Gary D 'Amato & Cliff Christl*
New York Yankees Trivia Teasers, *Richard Pennington*
Packers By the Numbers: Jersey Numbers and the Players Who Wore Them, *John Maxymuk*
Vagabond Halfback: The Life and Times of Johnny Blood McNally, *Denis J. Gullickson*

Gift Books

Madison, Photography by *Brent Nicastro*
Milwaukee, Photography by *Todd Dacquisto*
Spirit of the North: A Photographic Journey Through
Northern Wisconsin, *Richard Hamilton Smith*

Legends & Lore

Haunted Wisconsin, *Michael Norman and Beth Scott*
Hunting the American Werewolf, *Linda S. Godfrey*
Strange Wisconsin: More Badger State Weirdness, *Linda S. Godfrey*
The Beast of Bray Road: Tailing Wisconsin's Werewolf, *Linda S. Godfrey*
The Eagle's Voice: Tales Told by Indian Effigy Mounds, *Gary J. Maier, M.D.*
The Poison Widow: A True Story of Sin, Strychnine, & Murder, *Linda S. Godfrey*
The W-Files: True Reports of Wisconsin's Unexplained Phenomena, *Jay Rath*

For a free catalog, phone, write, or visit us online.

TRAILS BOOKS

A Division of Big Earth Publishing
923 Williamson Street, Madison, WI 53703
800.258.5830 · www.trailsbooks.com